I0759424

"Geoff Chang knows Charles Spurgeon well. As this work highlights, one of Spurgeon's grand themes throughout his ministry was suffering. This subject is often neglected, to our peril. Thankfully, Dr. Chang has brought Spurgeon's words to life again. We are the better for *Your Only Comfort*."

Brian Albert, Pastor, Calvary Baptist Church, Lenexa, KS

"Suffering is not an elective for the Christian. If we follow Jesus, it is a required course. As we traverse the dark valley, we need trusted friends to help us persevere. *Your Only Comfort* serves suffering believers by bringing them alongside the late great C. H. Spurgeon, who helps us honestly and hopefully lean on Jesus in affliction. Read and be encouraged to not lose heart!"

Garrett Kell, Pastor, Del Ray Baptist Church

"Spurgeon suffered terribly—both emotionally and physically—for nearly the entirety of his thirty-eight-year pastorate in London. Aware of the great suffering always afflicting many in the large crowds who heard him, Spurgeon often shared with them in preaching and in print the solid comforts he received from Christ and his Word. In these pages is a collection of some of his choicest words of consolation and encouragement. Sufferers today will find them as fresh and meaningful as they were in Spurgeon's day."

Donald S. Whitney, Professor of Biblical Spirituality,
John H. Powell Professor of Pastoral Ministry,
and Director of the Center for Biblical Spirituality,
Midwestern Baptist Theological Seminary; author
of *Spiritual Disciplines for the Christian Life*

"Charles Spurgeon was well acquainted with suffering. Debilitating health problems plagued him for most of his ministry, and he struggled frequently with deep depression. His wife was an invalid. And thousands of people who heard him preach sought his counsel when they faced loss or misery of various kinds. His sermons and writings are rich with warm-hearted, empathetic, biblical counsel for those who suffer. Geoff Chang has collected a month's worth of Spurgeon's most helpful and hopeful words. This is a priceless resource for anyone going through dark days."

Phil Johnson, Executive Director, Grace to You

Your Only Comfort

Your Only Comfort

Devotions for Hope in Suffering

CHARLES H. SPURGEON

EDITED BY GEOFFREY CHANG

New Growth Press, Greensboro, NC 27401
newgrowthpress.com

Cover Design: Faceout Books, faceoutstudio.com
Interior Design and Typesetting: Lisa Parnell, lparnellbookservices.com

ISBN: 978-1-64507-523-3 (hardcover)
ISBN: 978-1-64507-524-0 (ebook)

Library of Congress Cataloging-in-Publication Data on file

Printed in Canada

29 28 27 26 25 1 2 3 4 5

To my brothers and sisters
in the persecuted church.

1 Peter 5:10

Contents

Introduction

Nine large paintings line the walls of the Spurgeon Library on the campus of Midwestern Baptist Theological Seminary in Kansas City, Missouri. Together, they tell the story of Charles Haddon Spurgeon, the greatest preacher of the nineteenth century (1834–1892). They tell of his surprising conversion during a snowstorm under an unknown preacher; his decision to become a Baptist and pursue believer's baptism; his spectacular preaching ministry, which began at sixteen and once involved him preaching to over 23,000 people; his loving marriage to his dear wife Susannah; his expansive ministry in London, which involved overseeing two orphanages, leading the Pastors' College, and pastoring the largest evangelical church of his day, the Metropolitan Tabernacle. Alongside these paintings, visitors can see his massive pastoral library, his sixty-three volumes of published sermons, and all kinds of artifacts from his remarkable ministry. One could easily walk away with the impression that Spurgeon was some kind of pastoral superman.

But such an impression would be wrong. Spurgeon did not soar through his more than forty years of ministry. Rather, he mostly limped. The final painting in the room attempts to tell that story. There, Spurgeon is only in his fifties, but the pressures of ministry and illness have so aged him that he looks like he is in his sixties. He's supporting himself with a cane due to his gout. Instead of being in London, he is convalescing in Mentone, France, where he would regularly need to escape during winter months to try to recover his health. This painting is a reminder that suffering was not just a component of Spurgeon's life—it was the dark cloud that hung over all his labors and accomplishments.

The Suffering Pastor

Beginning in London in 1854 at the age of nineteen, Spurgeon threw himself into the work of ministry. The once dying New Park Street Chapel was quickly filled with hundreds of visitors, far beyond the building's capacity. Preaching invitations were pouring in for the young pastor, and in those early years, he preached as often as thirteen times a week. But preaching was only part of his work. He also pastored a church. He had prayer meetings to lead, services to plan, membership interviews to conduct, congregational meetings to chair, church members to visit, young men to disciple, elders and deacons to train, books to write, and much, much more. From the very beginning, Spurgeon bore a tremendous load.

And yet, amid these notable accomplishments, the strain of the ministry began to show. On October 19, 1856, Spurgeon preached for the first time at the Surrey Gardens Music Hall before an audience of ten thousand people. During the service, troublemakers caused a stampede as they gave coordinated shouts of "Fire!" In the ensuing panic, seven people were trampled to death, and dozens more were seriously injured. Spurgeon, in trying to restore order, collapsed and had to be carried out. In the following weeks, he fell into a dark depression. He would eventually recover, but the trauma of that night would remain with him for the rest of his life.

Beyond that harrowing event, the pressure and overwork would also quickly catch up with him. In the fall of 1858, Spurgeon found himself seriously ill and unable to preach for three consecutive Sundays. On his first Sunday back, he had to be carried up to the pulpit to preach. Clearly, he was not fully recovered. For the rest of his life, the combination of overwork and illness would become a pattern in his ministry. His doctors attributed his illness to kidney disease, which led to other painful ailments like gout and rheumatism. A friend once asked him what gout was like. Spurgeon responded, "If you put your hand into a vice and let a man press as hard as he can, that is rheumatism; and if he can be got to press a little harder, that is gout."[1] Gout would often lay him low, bringing sharp pain to his hands, feet, joints, lower back, muscles, and legs. At other times, he dealt with nerve pain, seizures, smallpox, sciatica, and other afflictions. As a preacher, Spurgeon carried all these ailments into the pulpit with him. For many weeks, his congregation received a visual sermon on suffering and perseverance as they watched their pastor preach through pain.

But Spurgeon's suffering was not limited to physical pain. Rather, the physical suffering often brought with it deep emotional pain. Doctors today might very well diagnose him with depression. But Spurgeon's experience of depression had a spiritual component to it. Amid his many

---

1. Jesse Page, *Spurgeon: His Life and Ministry* (London: S. W. Partridge & Co., 1903), 148.

illnesses, he often wrestled with doubts and fears. He once shared,

> I find that when I am in good physical health, I am not often tempted of Satan to despondency or doubt; but whenever I get depressed in spirit, or the liver is out of order, or the head aches, then comes the hissing serpent, "God has forsaken you, you are no child of God, you are unfaithful to your Master, you have no part in the blood of sprinkling," and such-like things. You old rascal! If you say as much as that to me in my days of health, when my blood is leaping in my veins, I shall be more than a match for you; but to meet me just then, when you understand that I am weak, ay! This is like you, Satan.[2]

Often, when battling illness, he wondered if he would ever be able to preach again. He feared becoming useless, a burden rather than a help. He could imagine his congregation suffering, the orphanage collapsing, and the college dissolving. All these anxieties only compounded his physical suffering with emotional dread and discouragement, leading to more physical weakness.[3] In his illness, he sometimes found himself in a dangerous spiral.

---

2. C. H. Spurgeon, *The Metropolitan Tabernacle Pulpit: Sermons Preached and Revised by C. H. Spurgeon,* Vols. 7–63 (London: Passmore & Alabaster, 1861–1917), 11:54.

3. "Mental depression tells upon the bodily frame . . . and is in itself the most painful of all diseases. Soul sickness tells upon the entire frame; it weakens the body, and then bodily weakness reacts upon the mind. . . . Deeper still the malady penetrates, till the bones, the more solid parts of the system, are affected." C. H. Spurgeon, *The Treasury of David* (New York: Funk and Wagnalls, 1892), 2:308.

As Spurgeon grew older, these afflictions would continue. But they were not his deepest sorrow. Rather, the most painful blow would come from the Downgrade Controversy (1887–1888). In that battle, Spurgeon confronted the theological liberalism that had infiltrated his denomination, the Baptist Union in England. Though its advocates claimed simply to modernize historic doctrines, he recognized that this "New Theology" was no Christianity at all.

> A new religion has been initiated, which is no more Christianity than chalk is cheese; and this religion, being destitute of moral honesty, palms itself off as the old faith with slight improvements, and on this plea usurps pulpits which were erected for gospel preaching. The Atonement is scouted, the inspiration of Scripture is derided, the Holy Spirit is degraded into an influence, the punishment of sin is turned into fiction, and the resurrection into a myth, and yet these enemies of our faith expect us to call them brethren, and maintain a confederacy with them![4]

Spurgeon attempted to sound the alarm, and when the Baptist Union refused to act, he withdrew from the denomination. For this, he was publicly denounced by the Union and attacked in the newspapers by fellow pastors and former allies. Many of his students refused to go along with him. In the end, he watched as his beloved denomination passed a declaration that did nothing to establish evangelical doctrines among its members. According to Susannah,

---

4. C. H. Spurgeon, "Another Word Concerning the Down-Grade," *The Sword and the Trowel: A Record of Combat with Sin & Labour for the Lord*, 37 vols. (London: Passmore & Alabaster, 1865–1902), August 1887: 397.

it was this conflict and the ensuing heartbreak that killed Spurgeon less than four years later.[5]

Learning from the Suffering Pastor

As we all know, suffering is part of life in a fallen world. To varying degrees, all of us will experience the futility of this life, which will eventually end in death. Suffering is God's loving warning to this world that something is wrong. We are separated from God because of our sin. But through the gospel, Jesus Christ, the Son of God, took upon himself our suffering humanity in order to reconcile us to the Father by bearing the judgment we deserve. For all who will repent of their rebellion and trust in Christ, their sins will be forgiven, and they will be restored to a right relationship with God.

But that doesn't mean suffering goes away for Christians. Rather, how we respond to suffering becomes a part of our witness. As Christians, it is in the middle of suffering that the truth of our hope shines brightest (1 Peter 3:14–15). We rejoice in the hope that God reigns over suffering (Romans 8:28) and that he uses suffering to refine and sanctify his people (James 1:2–4). We persevere in suffering, knowing that it is only momentary. There is an eternal weight of glory that awaits us (2 Corinthians 4:7).

Who better to help us in the middle of our own experiences of suffering than one of the greatest preachers of

5. C. H. Spurgeon, *C. H. Spurgeon's Autobiography: Compiled from His Diary, Letters, and Records, by His Wife, and His Private Secretary,* 4 vols. (London: Passmore & Alabaster, 1881–1894), 4:255.

church history, who himself knew deeply the pain and futility of this world? Who better to learn from than one who suffered physically, emotionally, spiritually, and relationally, and yet held steadfast to his hope in Christ? Receiving God's comfort from one another is part of his design, after all. As the apostle Paul writes, "[God] comforts us in all our affliction, so that we may be able to comfort those who are in any affliction, with the comfort with which we ourselves are comforted by God" (2 Corinthians 1:4).

On the first Sunday back in the pulpit after the Surrey Gardens Music Hall tragedy, Spurgeon entered the pulpit, broken and trembling. Standing before the congregation, all the trauma of that fateful night came back to him. He said to his people, "You will therefore excuse me this morning if I make no allusion to that solemn event, or scarcely any . . . I should be obliged to be silent if I should bring to my remembrance that terrific scene in the midst of which it was my solemn lot to stand." He shared with his people how he had struggled to find any comfort in God's Word during the previous weeks. But as his mind was tossed about by his troubles, there was a "single reflection [that] had such a power of comfort on [his] depressed spirit." This was the truth of the risen and exalted Christ:

> In the midst of calamities, whether they be the wreck of nations, the crash of empires, the heaving of revolutions, or the scourge of war, the great question which [the Christian] asks himself, and asks of others too, is this—Is Christ's kingdom safe? In his own personal afflictions his chief anxiety is—Will God be glorified, and will his honor be increased by it? If it be so, says he, although I be but

> as smoking flax, yet if the sun is not dimmed, I will rejoice, and though I be a bruised reed, if the pillars of the temple are unbroken, what matters it that my reed is bruised? . . . Amidst much tumult and divers rushings to and fro of troubling thoughts our souls have returned to the darling object of our desires, and we have found it no small consolation after all to say, "It matters not what shall become of us: God hath highly exalted him, and given him a name which is above every name: That at the name of Jesus every knee should bow."[6]

In his day, Spurgeon sought to teach his people about suffering. He preached about a Savior who was exalted above all and yet shared in their suffering. And he shared the comfort he himself had received with his congregation. This devotional draws from his many sermons on suffering to make that comfort available to a new generation so that we also might hold fast to Christ to the very end.

Geoffrey Chang
Kansas City, MO
June 11, 2024

6. C. H. Spurgeon, *The New Park Street Pulpit: Containing Sermons Preached and Revised by the Rev. C. H. Spurgeon, Minister of the Chapel*, 6 vols. (London: Passmore & Alabaster, 1855–1860.), 2:377.

Day 1

The Unchanging Christ

Jesus is the same yesterday and today and forever.
Hebrews 13:8

We are one day strong, and the next day weak—one day resolved, and the next day wavering—one hour constant, and the next hour unstable as water. We are one moment holy, kept by the power of God; we are the next moment sinning, led astray by our own lusts; but our Master is forever the same; pure, and never spotted; firm, and never changing—everlastingly Omnipotent, unchangeably Omniscient. From him, no attribute passes away.

Jesus Christ is the same with regard to his Father as ever. He was his Father's well-beloved Son before all worlds (John 15:5); he was his well-beloved in the stream of baptism (Matthew 3:17); he was his well-beloved on the cross (Isaiah 53:10); he was his well-beloved when he led captivity captive (Ephesians 4:8), and he is not less the object of his Father's infinite affection now than he was then. Yesterday he lay in Jehovah's bosom, God, having all power with his Father—today he stands on earth man, with us, but still the same, forever—he ascends on high and still he is his Father's Son still by inheritance, having a more excellent name than angels (Hebrews 1:4)—still sitting far above all principalities and powers, and every name that is named (Philippians 2:9–11). O Christian, give him your cause to plead; the Father will answer him as well now as he did before time. Doubt not the Father's grace. Go to your Advocate. He is as near to Jehovah's heart as ever—as prevalent in his intercession. Trust him, then, and in trusting him you may be sure of the Father's love for you.

But now there is a yet sweeter thought. Jesus Christ is the same to his people as ever. We have delighted in our happier moments, in days that have rolled away, to think of him that loved us when we had no being; we have often sung with rapture of him that loved us when we loved not him.

> Jesus sought me when a stranger,
> Wandering from the fold of God;
> He to save my soul from danger
> Interposed his precious blood.

We have looked back, too, upon the years of our troubles and our trials; and we can bear our solemn though humble witness, that he has been true to us in all our exigencies and has never failed us once. Come, then, let us comfort ourselves with this thought—that though today he may distress us with a sense of sin, yet his heart is just the same to us as ever. Christ may wear masks that look black to his people, but his face is always the same; Christ may sometimes take a rod in his hand instead of a golden scepter; but the name of his saints is as much engraved upon the hand that grasps the rod as upon the palm that clasps the scepter.

And oh, sweet thought that now bursts upon our mind! Beloved, you conceive how much Christ will love you when you are in heaven? Have you ever tried to fathom that bottomless sea of affection in which you shall swim, when you shall bathe yourself in seas of heavenly rest? Did you ever think of the love which Christ will manifest to you, when he shall present you without spot, or blemish, or any such thing, before his Father's throne? Well, pause and remember, that he loves you at this hour as much as he will love you then; for he will be the same forever as he is today, and he is the same today as he will be forever. This one thing I know: if Jesus's heart is set on me he will not love me one atom better when this head wears a crown, and when this hand shall with joyous fingers touch the strings of golden harps, than he does now, amidst all my sin and care and woe. I believe that saying which is written—"As the Father has loved me, so have I loved you" (John 15:9) and a higher degree of love we cannot imagine. The Father loves his Son infinitely, and even so today, believer, does the Son of God love you.

If he be the same today as yesterday, my soul, set not your affections upon these changing things, but set your heart upon him. O my heart, build not your house upon the sandy pillars of a world that soon must pass away, but build your hopes upon this rock, which when the rain descends and floods shall come, shall stand immovably secure. O my soul, I charge you, lay up your treasure in this secure granary. O my heart, I bid you now put your treasure where you can never lose it. Put it in Christ; put all your affections in his person, all your hope in his glory, all your trust in his efficacious blood, all your joy in his presence, and then you will have put yourself and put your all where you can never lose anything, because it is secure. Remember, O my heart, that the time is coming when all things must fade, and when you must part with all. Death's gloomy night must soon put out your sunshine; the dark flood must soon roll between you and all you have. Then put your heart with him who will never leave you and trust yourself with him who will go with you through the black and surging current of death's stream, and who will walk with you up the steep hills of heaven and make you sit together with him in heavenly places for ever.

Day 2
Thorns and Thistles

Cursed is the ground because of you;
in pain you shall eat of it all the days of your life;
thorns and thistles it shall bring forth for you;
and you shall eat the plants of the field.
By the sweat of your face
you shall eat bread,
till you return to the ground,
for out of it you were taken;
for you are dust,
and to dust you shall return.
Genesis 3:17–19

Ever since that first sin of our first parents, this has been generally true of the whole human race, not only of the earth literally, but of everything else round about us, "Thorns and thistles it shall bring forth to you."

It is so with regard to the natural world. This world is full of beauty; it is full of light; it yields a thousand pleasures; but still it is full of terror. There is much, indeed, to distress the frail mortals who live in this world. Have you ever been to sea in a storm? Have you not felt as if nature were at war with you then? Have you never been on the land in some tremendous thunderstorm, when the whole earth seemed to shake, and the skies were split with the fiery bolts? Ah, then you have felt that this world is not quite a paradise since man has become a sinner! The stars of heaven do not fight for him, but they sometimes fight against him. There are many things in this world, with its stern laws, that make it a place that has not all the comfort that a creature might wish. He is a sinful creature; and although he does not suffer all the discomfort that he deserves, yet this world is changed from what it was when God placed Adam in it to delight himself in paradise.

As it is in the natural world, so it is in the social world. You go out into the wide world of trade and business, and I think you find that it brings forth thorns and thistles to you. You do not have a week's dealing, a week's work, a week's going to and fro in this world without getting a pricking thorn here and there. If we do not all have to complain of this experience, I think we who are Christians will all admit that the world is not congenial to a believing man or woman. The society of the world is not helpful to a holy heart. To have to mix in it is rather a task, for which we need much grace, as we cry, "Lead us not into temptation, but deliver us from evil" (Matthew 6:13). You cannot have much to do with the men of the world without finding that many of them are sharper than a thorn hedge; and you cannot go to and fro in the earth without discovering that you are surrounded by those who make thorns and thistles to grow up all around you.

It is the same, also, in the religious world. The worst thorns and thistles that ever wound my heart are those that grow in religious circles. To see God's truth dishonored, to have the glory of Christ's substitution denied, to hear doctrines preached which would be novel if they were not old errors new vamped, and brought forth from the oblivion in which they deserved to rot, and to see Christian people behave themselves as some of them do, having little respect to the name of him whom they profess to serve, and bringing discredit on the sacred cause for which they ought to be willing to die rather than to cast a slur upon it, these are thorns and thistles that pierce us to the very heart.

I will go a little further, and tread upon delicate ground. I am afraid that many of you have felt that, even in the little family world in which you move, you are not left without trials. God, when he took away paradise as our home, gave us home to be our paradise; and if there be a place where all felicities are to be found, it is around the family hearth. Yet where is there a home without affliction? The dear child whom you love sickens and dies; perhaps the wife or the husband may be taken away to the long home; or poverty comes in; or one whom you love dearer than yourself pines daily with constant sickness and frequent agony. No, we must not expect perfect peace, perfect felicity, even in the home which is blessed with morning and evening prayer, where God locks up the door at night and draws the curtains in the morning; no, not even there, my dear friends, shall we be free from the curse that sin brought into this fair world.

And it is so if you get a little closer home still, to the microcosm or little world of your own self. There is no part of man which does not yield him its thorns. Many of us have a thorn in the flesh (2 Corinthians 12:7). Is there any part of the body which may not, if God so wills it, become the subject of disease, and consequently the source of pain to us? I know some whom God dearly loves—I know he loves them, for he favors them very highly—who nevertheless find that in the body of this flesh there are the seeds of corruption. There are the bitter wells of Marah (Exodus 15:23) by reason of sharp pain of body; and as to the mind itself, what mind is there that is fullest of faith, and most joyful in the Lord, which is not naturally still the subject of grief?

Yes, and even in the soul itself, by reason of the imperfection of our sanctification, from the fact that we are not so filled by the Spirit, and not so conscious of the abiding of the Spirit within us as we yet shall be, thorns also and thistles are brought forth to us. I may be speaking to some who can say, with an emphasis, that they oftentimes find great crops of thistles springing up in their hearts, and they have to keep the sickle of sacred mortification going to cut them down, and they try if possible to dig them up by the roots. But thus it is; you cannot expect a perfect life of happiness in an imperfect world like this. No; your Savior carried the cross, and you will have a cross of some kind or other to carry after him. "Thorns and thistles it shall bring forth to you."

Day 3
Divine Sovereignty

Am I not allowed to do what I choose
with what belongs to me?
Matthew 20:15

The householder says, "Is it not lawful for me to do what I will with my own?" and even so does the God of heaven and earth ask this question of you this morning, "Is it not lawful for me to do what I will with my own?" There is no attribute of God more comforting to his children than the doctrine of Divine Sovereignty. Under the most adverse circumstances, in the most severe troubles, they believe that Sovereignty hath ordained their afflictions, that Sovereignty overrules them, and that Sovereignty will sanctify them all. There is nothing for which the children of God ought more earnestly to contend than the dominion of their Master over all creation—the kingship of God over all the works of his own hands—the throne of God, and his right to sit upon that throne.

On the other hand, there is no doctrine more hated by worldlings, no truth of which they have made such a football, as the great, stupendous, but yet most certain doctrine of the Sovereignty of the infinite Jehovah. Men will allow God to be everywhere except on his throne. They will allow him to be in his workshop to fashion worlds and to make stars. They will allow him to be in his charity to dispense his alms and bestow his bounties. They will allow him to sustain the earth and bear up the pillars thereof, or light the lamps of heaven, or rule the waves of the ever-moving ocean; but when God ascends his throne, his creatures then gnash their teeth; and when we proclaim an enthroned God, and his right to do as he wills with his own, to dispose of his creatures as he thinks well, without consulting them in the matter, then it is that we are hissed and execrated, and then it is that men turn a deaf ear to us, for God on his throne is not the God they love. They love him anywhere better than they do when he sits with his scepter in his hand and his crown upon his head. But it is God upon the throne that we love to preach. It is God upon his throne whom we trust.

It is an indisputable fact that God has not, in temporal matters, given to every man alike; that he has not distributed to all his creatures the same amount of happiness or the same standing in creation. There is a difference. Mark what a difference there is in men personally; one is born like Saul a head and shoulders taller than the rest (1 Samuel 9:2)—another shall live all his life a Zaccheus—a man short of stature (Luke 19:2–3). One has a muscular frame and a share of beauty—another is weak, and far from having anything styled comeliness. How many do we find whose eyes have never rejoiced in the sunlight, whose ears have never listened to the charms of music, and whose lips have never been moved to sounds intelligible or harmonious? Walk through the earth and you will find men superior to yourself in vigor, health, and fashion, and others who are your inferiors in the very same respects. Some here are preferred far above their fellows in their outward appearance, and some sink low in the scale and have nothing about them that can make them glory in the flesh.

Why has God given to one man beauty and to another none; to one all his senses, and to another but a portion?

The disciples asked, "Who sinned, this man or his parents, that he was born blind?" (John 9:2). We know that there was neither sin in parents nor child, that he was born blind, or that others have suffered similar distresses, but that God has done as it has pleased him in the distribution of his earthly benefits, and thus hath said to the world, "Is it not lawful for me to do what I will with my own?"

Note again, the Divine Sovereignty, in that God chose the Israelite race and left the Gentiles for years in darkness. Why was Israel instructed and saved, while Syria was left to perish in idolatry? Was the one race purer in its origin and better in its character than the other? Did not the Israelites take unto themselves false gods a thousand times, and provoke the true God to anger and loathing? Why then, should they be favored above their fellows? Why did the sun of heaven shine upon them while all around the nations were left in darkness, and were sinking into hell by myriads? Why?

The only answer that can be given is this, that God is a Sovereign, and "has mercy upon whomever he wills, and hardens whomever he wills" (Romans 9:18). So now, also, why is it that God sent his word to us while a multitude of people are still without his word? Why do we each come up to God's tabernacle, Sabbath after Sabbath, privileged to listen to the voice of the minister of Jesus, while other nations have not been visited thereby? Could not God have caused the light to shine in the darkness there as well as here? Could not he, if he had pleased, have sent forth messengers swift as the light to proclaim his gospel over the whole earth? He could have done it if he would. Since we know that he has not done it, we bow in meekness, confessing his right to do as he wills with his own.

We must trace, I say, Divine Sovereignty in all such cases. We ought to recognize God's hand in everything. But the present is the most godless generation that ever trod this earth, I verily believe. In our fathers' days there was hardly a shower but they declared that God caused it to fall; and they had prayers for rain, prayers for sunshine, and prayers for harvest; as well when a haystack was on fire, as when a famine desolated the land; our forefathers said, the Lord hath done it. But now our philosophers try to explain everything, and trace all phenomena to second causes. But brethren, let it be ours to ascribe the origin and direction of all things to the Lord, and the Lord alone.

Day 4
Accidents, Not Punishments

Or those eighteen on whom the tower in Siloam fell and killed them: do you think that they were worse offenders than all the others who lived in Jerusalem? No, I tell you; but unless you repent, you will all likewise perish.
Luke 13:4–5

This sermon was preached after the Clayton Tunnel crash, which took place on August 25, 1861. At the time, it was the worst accident on the British railway system, killing 23 and injuring 176 passengers.

In reading the newspapers during the last two weeks, even the most stolid must have been the subject of very painful feelings. Not only have there been catastrophes so alarming that the blood chills at their remembrance, but column after column of the paper has been devoted to calamities of a minor degree of horror, but which, when added together, are enough to astound the mind with the fearful amount of sudden death which has of late fallen on the sons of men. We have had not only one incident for every day in the week, but two or three; we have not simply been stunned with the alarming noise of one terrific clash, but another, and another, and another, have followed upon each other's heels, like Job's messengers, till we have needed Job's patience and resignation to hear the dreadful tale of woes.

Now, men and brethren, such things as these have always happened in all ages of the world. Think not that this is a new thing; do not dream, as some do, that this is the produce of an overwrought civilization, or of that modern and most wonderful discovery of steam. If the steam engine had never been known, and if the railway had never been constructed, there would have been sudden deaths and terrible accidents, notwithstanding. Be not, therefore, cast down with any sudden fear, neither be troubled by these calamities. Go about your business, and if your avocations should call you to cross the field of death itself, do it, and do it bravely. God has not thrown up the reins of the world, he has not taken off his hand from the helm of the great ship. Only learn to trust him, and you shall not be afraid of sudden fear; "hissoul shall dwell at ease; and his seed shall inherit the earth" (Psalm 25:13 KJV).

It has been most absurdly stated that those who travel on the first day of the week and meet with an accident, ought to regard that accident as being a judgment from God upon them on account of their violating the Christian's day of worship. It has been stated even by godly ministers, that the late deplorable collision should be looked upon as an exceedingly wonderful and remarkable visitation of the wrath of God against those unhappy persons who happened to be in the Clayton tunnel. Now I enter my solemn protest against such an inference as that, not in my own name, but in the name of Him who is the Christian's Master and the Christian's Teacher. I say of those who were crushed in that tunnel, do you think that they were sinners above all the sinners? "No, I tell you; but unless you repent, you will all likewise perish." Or those who perished but last Monday, do you think that they were sinners above all the sinners that were in London? "No, I tell you; but unless you repent, you will all likewise perish."

Now, mark, I would not deny but what there have sometimes been judgments of God upon particular persons for sin; sometimes, and I think but exceedingly rarely, such things have occurred. But in cases of accident, such as that to which I refer, and in cases of sudden and instant death, again, I say, I enter my earnest protest against the foolish and ridiculous idea that those who thus perish are sinners above all the sinners who survive unharmed. Let us take heed that we do not draw the rash and hasty conclusion from terrible accidents that those who suffer by them suffer on account of their sins.

Do you not perceive that such an idea as this would encourage Phariseeism? These people who were crushed to death, scalded, or destroyed under the wheels of railway carriages, were worse sinners than we are. Very well, then what good people we must be; what excellent examples of virtue! We do not such things as they, and therefore God makes all things smooth for us. Inasmuch as we here traveled some of us every day in the week, and yet have never been smashed to pieces, we may on this supposition rank ourselves with the favorites of Deity.

But I cannot indulge this for a moment. As I look for a moment upon the poor mangled bodies of those who have been so suddenly slain, my eyes find tears, but my heart does not boast, nor my lips accuse. While we can thank God that we are preserved, yet we can say, "It is of the Lord's mercies that we are not consumed," (Lamentations 3:22 KJV) and we must ascribe it to his grace, and to his grace alone. It is only because he has had mercy, and been very long-suffering toward us, not willing that we should perish, but that we should come to repentance (2 Peter 3:9), that he has thus preserved us from going down to the grave, and kept us alive from death.

Instead of thinking of their sins which would make me proud, I should think of my own which will make me humble. Instead of speculating upon their guilt, which is no business of mine, I should turn my eyes within and think upon my own transgression, for which I must personally answer before the Most High God. Then the next question is: Have I repented of my sin? I need not be inquiring whether they have or not: have I? Since I am liable to the same calamity, am I prepared to meet it? Do I hate sin? Have I learned to abhor it? Have I, through the Holy Spirit, turned away from it as from a deadly poison, and do I seek now to honor Christ, my Master? Am I washed in his blood? Do I bear his likeness? Do I reflect his character? Do I seek to live to his praise? For if not, I am in as great danger as they were, and may quite as suddenly be cut off, and then where am I? Am I prepared to die? If now the gates of hell should be opened, shall I enter there? If now beneath me the wide jaws of death should gape, am I prepared with confidence to walk through the midst of them, fearing no evil, because God is with me?

This is the proper use to make of these accidents; this is the wisest way to apply the judgments of God to our own selves and to our own condition.

Day 5

Deep Calls to Deep

Deep calls to deep
at the roar of your waterfalls;
all your breakers and your waves
have gone over me.
Psalm 42:7

What a depth! What an inscrutable mystery, that the infinitely pure and holy God should have determined to allow the intrusion of sin into his universe; that he should suffer evil to drag down an angel and debase him into a devil; that the adoring hosts of heaven should be thinned by sinful desertion from a loyalty so well deserved! How came it that moral evil was suffered to come into this fair world, to spoil Eden, to pollute mankind, to fill the grave, and populate hell? Why was it that after sin had broken out in the universe, it was permitted to remain in existence? Why not shut up the first devil as in a plague ward, environ it with walls of flame, and never let the demon wander forth? Why should the evil one be permitted like a roaring lion to roam abroad seeking whom he may devour? When sin infected the race of men, why not destroy them all and stamp out the disease, as we did lately when the disease came among our cattle? Why not purge with fire till the last speck of the leprosy was burned out? What mattered the destruction of a race if sin were but destroyed with them? Strange decree that sin should be tolerated; permitted first to enter, and then allowed afterwards to spread its mischievous poison.

What a depth, my brethren, is revealed in the divine decree of election, that there should be vessels unto honor, fitted for the Master's use, men chosen to show forth the riches of his grace, not for any good thing in them, but because the Lord will have mercy upon whom he will have mercy, and will have compassion on whom he will have compassion. And what a depth more solemn still, is revealed in those whom he passed by; that there should be vessels of wrath fitted to destruction, men permitted to continue in sin and to harden themselves against the gospel, and so to illustrate the awful wrath of God throughout eternity. Brethren, I cannot contemplate the doctrines connected with predestination, true as they are, without a shudder of reverential awe. Read that ninth chapter of the Romans, and while you are silenced by the voice of Paul, "But who are you, O man, to answer back to God? Will what is molded say to its molder, 'Why have you made me like this?'" (Romans 9:20). Yet, a thrill of awe passes through your souls, and you whisper—

Great God, how infinite art thou,
What worthless worms are we!

If we could turn over those awful pages in which every event has been recorded, if it were permitted to us to see that book of fate chained to the throne of God, in which every angel's form and size is drawn by the eternal pen, in which everything is written down from the falling of a sere leaf from an oak to the tumbling of an avalanche from its Alp, in which God has as much arranged the course of yonder dust blown in the wind as of the planet which he steers in its mighty orbit; if we could see it all, we should exclaim, "O wondrous depth, how can I measure you? My plummet utterly fails. I will adore, for I cannot comprehend."

Beloved friends, we need not allow ourselves to be depressed by the mystery of the doctrine of eternal decrees, for even if these decrees were not in existence, there would still remain the other deep, the mystery of fact. It is a fact that sin is in the world; it is a fact that sorrow is there; it is a fact that death is there; and how can you understand these things? Shut your eye to the depth above the firmament if you will, but here is depth nearer home which will still amaze you.

Remember that all men are not saved. It is a dreadful truth that multitudes tread the broad road and reach eternal destruction (Matthew 7:13). Why is this when God is good and omnipotent? Can you understand providence? Is not providence, as we see it, quite as mysterious as predestination? Are not the mysteries rather in the facts themselves than in the purposes which ordained them? Are they not, both the facts and the decrees, mysteries and equal mysteries? But what a wonderful harmony there is between the two depths! And this I call your attention. Observe how deep has called unto deep. Whatsoever God ordained has been accomplished; his will has been done. You will tell me that this is nothing wonderful, since God is omnipotent. I reply, yes; but you will remember that he was pleased to create beings who should be free agents, and to that extent actors independent of himself. Therefore, it is not to the solitary attribute of omnipotence that you can refer the fact that providence coincides with predestination. Here were angels free in their will, and yet they sinned.

Here are men upon this stage of action willful and resolute, and yet fulfilling the unknown fore-ordination. Herein lies the marvel, that with voluntary agents, who do as they will, yet the eternal purpose in every jot and tittle has to this moment been fulfilled; and as the impression answers to the die, so has the history of the universe answered to the eternal purpose, and to the solemn decree of the Most High. My brethren, in solemn awe listen to the voices of these twin depths as they call to one another. Famine, plague, pestilence, devastated nations, fallen empires, wars, and bloodsheds, who shall understand why these are permitted? How shall we reconcile our souls to them at all, until we look up to the great Father sitting on the throne of wisdom and love, and say, "You know what the end will be. You have ordained all things, and from the seeming evil you will bring forth good, and from the good a something better, and from the better something better still, in infinite progression, to the praise and glory of your name?"

"Deep calls unto deep." The deep of predestination answers to the deep of providence, and both together magnify the name of God.

Day 6
If the Lord Wills

Come now, you who say, "Today or tomorrow
we will go into such and such a town and spend a year
there and trade and make a profit"—yet you do not know
what tomorrow will bring. What is your life? For you
are a mist that appears for a little time and then vanishes.
Instead you ought to say, "If the Lord wills,
we will live and do this or that."
James 4:13–15

Men today are just the same as when these words were first written. We still find people saying what they are going to do today, tomorrow, or in six months' time, at the end of another year, and perhaps still further. I have no doubt there are persons here who have their own career mapped out before them pretty distinctly, and they feel well-nigh certain that they will realize it all. We are like the men of the past; and this Book, though it has been written so long, might have been written yesterday, so exactly does it describe human nature as it is at the end of this nineteenth century.

The apostle, by the Spirit, speaks truly when he says, "You do not know what tomorrow will bring." Whether it will come to us laden with sickness or health, prosperity or adversity, we cannot tell. Tomorrow may mark the end of our life; possibly even the end of the age. Our ignorance of the future is certainly a fact. Only God knows the future. All things are present to him; there is no past and no future to his all-seeing eyes. He dwells in the present tense evermore as the great I AM. He knows what will be on the morrow, and he alone knows. The whole course of the universe lies before him, like an open map. Men do not know what a day may bring forth, but Jehovah knows the end from the beginning. There are two great certainties about things that shall come to pass—one is that God knows, and the other is that we do not know.

What says our text? "Instead you ought to say, 'If the Lord wills, we will live and do this or that.'" I do not think that we need always, in every letter and in every handbill, put "If the Lord wills"; yet I wish that we oftener used those very words. The fashionable way is to put it in Latin, and even then to abbreviate it, and use only the consonants "D.V."[1] to express it. You know, it is a fine thing when you can put your religion into Latin and make it very short. Then nobody knows what you mean by it; or, if they do, they can praise your scholarship, and admire your humility.

I do not care about those letters "D.V." I rather like what Fuller says when he describes himself as writing in the letter such passages as "God willing," or "God lending me life." He says, "I observe, Lord, that I can scarcely hold my hand from encircling these words in parenthesis, as if they were not essential to the sentence, but may as well be left out as put in. Whereas, indeed, they are not only of the commission at large, but so of the quorum, that without them all the rest is nothing; wherefore hereafter, I will write these words freely and fairly, without any enclosure about them. Let critics censure it for bad grammar, I am sure it is good divinity." So he quaintly puts the matter. Still, whether

1. *Deo volente*, which is Latin for "God willing."

you write, "If the Lord will," or not, always let it be clearly understood; and let it be conspicuous in all your arrangements that you recognize that God is over all, and that you are under his control. When you say, "I will do this or that," always add, in thought if not in word, "If the Lord will." No harm can come to you if you bow to God's sovereign sway.

May this be your resolve, then; let this clause, "if the Lord will," be written across your life, and let us all set ourselves to the recognition of God in the future. It is a grand thing to be able to say, "Wherever I go, and whatever happens to me, I belong to God; and I can say that God will prepare my way as well when I am old and gray-headed as he did when I was a boy. He shall guide me all the way to my everlasting mansion in glory; he was the guide of my youth; he shall be the guide of my old age. I will leave everything to him, all the way from earth to heaven; and I will be content to live only a day at a time; and my happy song shall be—

So for tomorrow and its need I do not pray,
But keep me, guide me, hold me, Lord,
Just for today.

Day 7
Job's Worship

Then Job arose and tore his robe and shaved his head and fell on the ground and worshiped.
Job 1:20

Job was very much troubled, and he did not try to hide the outward signs of his sorrow. A man of God is not expected to be a stoic. The grace of God takes away the heart of stone out of his flesh (Ezekiel 36:26), but it does not turn his heart into a stone. The Lord's children are the subjects of tender feelings; when they have to endure the rod, they feel the pain of its strokes; and Job felt the blows that fell upon him.

Do not blame yourself if you are conscious of pain and grief, and do not ask to be made hard and callous. That is not the method by which grace works; it makes us strong to bear trial, but we have to bear it; it gives us patience and submission, not stoicism. We feel, and we benefit by the feeling, and there is no sin in the feeling, for in our text we are expressly told of the patriarch's mourning, "In all this Job sinned not." Though he was the great mourner—I think I might truly call him the chief mourner—of Scripture, yet there was no sin in his mourning. Some there are who say that, when we are heavy of heart, we are necessarily in a wrong spirit, but it is not so. The apostle Peter says, "If necessary, you have been grieved by various trials" (1 Peter 1:6), but he does not imply that the heaviness is wrong. There are some who will not cry when God chastises them, and some who will not yield when God smites them. We do not wish to be like them; we are quite content to have the suffering heart that Job had, and to feel the bitterness of spirit, the anguish of soul which racked that blessed patriarch.

Furthermore, Job made use of very manifest signs of mourning. He not only felt sorrow within his heart, but he indicated it by rending his mantle, by shaving off the hair of his head, and by casting himself prone upon the ground, as if he sought to return to the womb of mother-earth as he said that he should; and I do not think we are to judge those of our brethren and sisters who feel it right to wear the common tokens of mourning. If they give them any kind of solace in their sorrow, let them have them. I believe that, at times, some go to excess in this respect, but I dare not pass sentence upon them because I read here, "In all this Job sinned not, nor charged God foolishly." I remember the gentleness of Jesus towards mourners rather than his severity in dealing with them; he has much pity for our weakness, and I wish that some of his servants had more of the same spirit.

I want you, however, to notice that mourning should always be sanctified with devotion. It is very pleasant to observe that, when Job had rent his mantle after the Oriental custom, and shaved his head, and, after the patriarch had fallen down upon the ground, he "worshipped." Not, he grumbled; not, he lamented; much less that he began to imprecate and use language unjustifiable and improper; but he "fell down upon the ground, and worshipped." O dear friend, when your grief presses you to the very dust, worship there! If that spot has come to be your Gethsemane, then present there your "loud cries and tears" (Hebrews 5:7) unto your God. Remember David's words, "O people, pour out your heart before him; God is a refuge for us" (Psalm 62:8). When you are bowed down beneath a heavy burden of sorrow, then take to worshipping the Lord, and especially to that kind of worshipping which lies in adoring God, and in making a full surrender of yourself to the divine will, so that you can say with Job, "Though he slay me, I will hope in him" (Job 13:15). That kind of worshipping which lies in the subduing of the will, the arousing of the affections, the bestirring of the whole mind and heart, and the presentation of oneself unto God over again in solemn consecration, must tend to sweeten sorrow, and to take the sting out of it.

It will also greatly alleviate our sorrow if we then fall into serious contemplations, and begin to argue a little, and to bring facts to bear upon our mind. Evidently, Job did so, for these verses are full of proofs of his thoughtfulness. In like manner, you will do well, not merely to sit still and say, "I shall be comforted," but you must look about you for themes upon which to think and meditate to profit. Your poor mind is apt to be driven to and fro by stress of your sorrow; if you can get anchor-hold of some great clearly ascertained truths, about which you can have no possible doubt, you may begin to derive consolation from them. "As I mused," said David, "the fire burned" (Psalm 39:3), and it comforted and warmed him. Remember how he talked to himself as to another self, "Why are you cast down, O my soul, and why are you in turmoil within me? Hope in God; for I shall again praise him, my salvation and my God" (Psalm 42:11). There are two Davids, you see, talking to one another, and cheering one another! A man ought always to be good company for himself, and he ought also to be able to catechize himself; he who is not fit to be his own schoolmaster is not fit to be schoolmaster to other people. If you cannot catechize your own heart, and drill a truth into your own soul, you do not know how to teach other people. I believe that the best preaching in the world is that which is done at home. When a sorrowing spirit shall have comforted itself, it will have learned the art of consoling other people. Job is an instance of this kind of personal instruction.

Day 8
Job's Confession

And he said, "Naked I came from my mother's womb, and naked shall I return. The Lord gave, and the Lord has taken away; blessed be the name of the Lord."
Job 1:21

We are then, first of all, to behold God's hand as a giving hand. If we are believers, all the comforts and mercies that we have are to be viewed by us as coming from the hand of our gracious Heavenly Father. Job confessed that the Lord had given him the camels, and the sheep, and the oxen, and that the Lord had given him his seven sons and three daughters; everything which he had ever possessed he looked upon as having been the gift of God. Job did not say, "I worked hard to obtain all that stock that I have now lost." He did not complain, "I spent many weary days and many anxious nights in accumulating all those flocks and herds that have been stolen from me." He did not ascribe any of his wealth either to his own wit, or to his own industry, but he said of it all, "The Lord gave it to me." In his mind's eye, he took an inventory of all that he once had, and of all that he had lost, and he said of the whole, "It was all the Lord's gift to me."

Now, beloved, whatever may be the possessions which you have at the present time, whatever may be the number of those who are the comfort of your life, husband or wife, parents or children, kinsfolk of any sort—say of all of them, "The Lord gave them to me"; and, as a Christian, learn the wisdom of never ascribing any earthly comfort to any earthly source. The believer in Christ may say, with the utmost truthfulness, with regard to all that he has, "It is all the gift of my loving and tender Heavenly Father." And, brethren, there is associated with this fact that all our possessions are God's gifts, the remembrance that they are all undeserved gifts. They are gifts in the fullest sense of the word, the gifts of God's grace. They are not given to us because we have merited them, for we have never deserved even the least of all the mercies which the Lord has so bountifully bestowed upon us. All that we have, over and above what would have been our portion in the pit of hell, is the gift of God's mercy towards us.

But now we are to think, for a while, of the Lord's hand taking away from us as well as giving to us. Job said, "The Lord gave, and the Lord hath taken away." Some of you have come to this service very sad and heavy of heart because that dear child of yours is dead. Well, I do not blame you for sorrowing over your loss, but I pray you also to remember that it is the Lord who has taken your child away from you. You say that it was the fever that took away your dear one, and perhaps that was the immediate cause of your child's death; but if you can realize that the fever was only the instrument in God's hand to remove the dear little one from your care to his own, surely you will dry your tears. And as for that substance of yours, which has almost melted away under the fiery trial to which it has been subjected, so that poverty now to stare you in the face, you will be able to bear even that when you remember that it is the Lord's hand that has taken away what his hand had first given.

So long as we look at the secondary causes of our trouble, we have reasons for sorrow; but when our faith can pierce the veil, and see the Great First Cause, then our comfort begins. If you strike a dog with a stick, he will try to bite the stick, because he is a dog; but if he knew better, he would try to bite you, and not the stick. Yet that is the way that we often act with the troubles that come to us; we fly at the second causes, and so are angry and petulant with them; but if we would always recollect that it is God who takes away, as well as God who gives—that he is at the back of all our trials and troubles—that his hand weighs out our shame of grief, and measures our portion of pain, then we should not dare to rebel and bewail; but, like David, we should say, "I am mute; I do not open my mouth, for it is you who have done it" (Psalm 39:9); even if we could not get up higher still, and say, with Job, "The Lord giveth, and the Lord taketh away; blessed be the name of the Lord."

Further, when once we know that God has done anything, that fact forbids any question concerning it. It must be right because he did it; I may not be able to tell why, but God knows why he did it. He may not tell me the reason; but he has a reason, for the Lord never acted unreasonably. There never was any action of his, however sovereign or autocratic it might appear to be, but was done "according to the counsel of his will" (Ephesians 1:11). Infinite wisdom dictates what absolute sovereignty decrees. God is never arbitrary, or tyrannical. He does as he wills, but he always wills to do that which is not only most, for his own glory, but also most for our real good (Romans 8:28). How dare we question anything that God does?

If health and wealth were good things for you, God would let you have them. If it were a good thing for saints never to die, they never would die. If it were a good thing for them to go to heaven at once, they would go there at once. If you are walking uprightly, you may know that you have all things, which, all things considered, would be good for you. Some things, which might be good in themselves, or good for others, might not be good for you; and, therefore, the Lord in love withholds them from you. But, whatever he gives, or takes away, or withholds, raise no questions concerning it, but let it be sufficient for you that the Lord has done it.

Day 9

Job's Regret and Our Own

"Oh, that I were as in the months of old,
as in the days when God watched over me,
when his lamp shone upon my head,
and by his light I walked through darkness,
as I was in my prime,
when the friendship of God was upon my tent
Job 29:2–4

We have a universal tendency to undervalue the present and exaggerate the excellence of the past. Have you never noticed this in natural things, we are prone to cast a partial eye upon some imaginary "good old times?" It is gone, and therefore it was good; it is here, and therefore it is dubious. In the middle of the summer, we feel that the heat is so relaxing that a frost would be the most delightful thing conceivable; we love, we say, the bracing air of winter; we are sure it is much healthier for us; yet, usually, when winter arrives, and the extreme cold sets in, we are all most anxious for the advent of spring, and we feel that somehow or other the frost is more trying to us than the heat. The fact is that whatever is with us we think to be the worse, and whatever was with us we conceive to be the better. We may, therefore, take some discount from our regrets; for, peradventure, were we more conscious of the benefit of the present state, and did we make less prominent the difficulty of it, we should not sigh to be as we were in months past.

Then, again, regrets may in some cases arise from a holy jealousy. The Christian, in whatever state he is, feels his own imperfection much, and laments his conscious shortcomings. Looking back, he observes with joy the work of grace in his soul, and does not perhaps so readily recollect the then existing deficiencies of nature; hence, he comes to think that the past was better than the present. He is afraid of backsliding, and therefore he jealously fears that he is so; he is so anxious to live nearer to God, so dissatisfied with his present attainments, that he dares not believe that he advances, but fears that he has lost ground.

I know this in my own experience, for when lying sick I have frequently lamented that pain has distracted my mind, and taken off my attention from the word of God, and I have longed for those seasons of health when I could read, meditate, and study with pleasure; but, now that I have risen up from the sickbed, and am growing strong again, I frequently look back to the long nights and quiet days spent in my sick chamber, and think that it was better with me then than now, for now I am apt to be cumbered with much serving, and then I was shut in with God.

Many a man is really strong in Christ; but, because he does not feel all the juvenile vivacity of his early days, he fears that ritual dullness has come upon him. He is now far more solid and steadfast, if not quite so quick and impulsive; but, the good man in his holy jealousy marks most the excellencies of his juvenile piety, and forgets that there were grave deficiencies in it; while, in his present state, he notes the deficiencies, and fears to hope that he possesses any excellencies. We are poor judges of our own condition, and usually err on one side or the other.

And, let me add, that very often these regrets of ours about the past are not wise. It is impossible to draw a fair comparison between the various stages of Christian experience, so as to give a judicious preference to one above another. Consider, as in a parable, the seasons of the year. There are many persons who, in the midst of the beauties of spring, say, "Ah, but how fitful is the weather! These March winds and April showers come and go by such fits and starts, that nothing is to be depended upon. Give me the safer glories of summer." Yet, when they feel the heat of summer, and wipe the sweat from their brows, they say, "After all, with all the full-blown beauty around us, we admire more the freshness, verdure, and vivacity of spring. The snowdrop and the crocus, coming forth as the advance guard of the army of flowers, have a superior charm about them." Now it is idle to compare spring with summer; they differ, and have each its beauties. We are in autumn now, and very likely, instead of prizing the peculiar treasures of autumn, some will despise the peaceful Sabbath of the year, and mournfully compare your fading leaves to funeral sermons replete with sadness. Such will contrast summer and autumn, and exalt one above another.

Now, whoever shall claim precedence for any season, shall have me for an opponent. They are all beautiful in their season, and each excels after its kind. Even thus it is wrong to compare the early zeal of the young Christian with the mature and mellow experience of the older believer, and make preferences. Each is beautiful according to its time. You, dear young friend, with your intense zeal, are to be commended and imitated; but very much of your fire I am afraid arises from novelty, and you are not so strong as you are earnest; like a newborn river, you are swift in current, but neither deep nor broad. And you, my more advanced friend, who are much tried and buffeted, to you it is not easy to hold on your way under great inward struggles and severe depressions, but your deeper sense of weakness, your firmer grasp of truth, your more intense fellowship with the Lord Jesus in his sufferings, your patience, and your steadfastness, are all lovely in the eyes of the Lord your God. Be thankful each of you for what you have, for by the grace of God you are what you are.

Day 10
Sweet Medicine for the Fainting Soul

My soul is cast down within me;
therefore I remember you
from the land of Jordan and of Hermon,
from Mount Mizar.
Psalm 42:6

The real reason of the psalmist's distress was, no doubt, that God had, at least to some degree, hidden his face from him, and therefore the flowers of his graces all drooped, and his joy, which erstwhile did sparkle in the sunlight of God's countenance, was now dim and dark.

The causes of our being cast down are very numerous. Sometimes, it is pain of body; peradventure, a wearing pain, which tries the nerves, prevents sleep, distracts our attention, drives away comfort, and hides contentment from our eyes. Often, too, has it been debility of body; some secret disease has been sapping and undermining the very strength of our life, and we knew not that it was there, while we have been drawing nigh insensibly to the gates of death. We have wondered that we were low in spirits, whereas it would have been a thousand wonders if we had not been depressed. We have marveled that we have been cast down, whereas the physician would tell us that this was but one of many symptoms which proved that we were not right as to our bodily health.

Not infrequently has some crushing calamity been the cause of depression of spirit. Trial has succeeded trial, all your hopes have been blasted, your very means of sustenance have been suddenly snatched from you; while all your needs have remained, the supplies have been withdrawn from you. At other times, it has been bereavement that has brought you down very low. The axe has been at work in the forest of your domestic joys. Tree after tree has fallen; those from whom you plucked the ripest fruits of sweet society and kindred fellowship have been cut down by the ruthless woodsman; you have seen them taken away from you forever so far as this world is concerned.

Or else it may be that you have been slandered; your good has been evil spoken of, your holiest motives have been misinterpreted, your divinest aspirations have been misrepresented, and you have gone about as with a sword in your bone while the malicious have taunted you, saying, "Where is now your God?" (Psalm 42:3).

The cases of depression of spirit are so various that it must be indeed a rare panacea, a marvelous remedy, which would suit them all. Yet, when we come to speak of the remedies mentioned in our text, we shall find them suitable to most of these cases, if not to all—and to all in a degree, if not to the fullest extent.

The first remedy for soul-dejection is a reference of ourselves to God, as David says, "O my God, my soul is cast down within me; therefore I remember you." If you have a trouble to bear, the best thing for you to do is not to try to bear it at all, but to cast it upon the shoulders of the Eternal. If you have anything that perplexes you, the simplest plan for you will be, not to try to solve the difficulty, but to seek direction from heaven concerning it. If you have, at this moment, some doubt that is troubling you, your wisest plan will be, not to combat the doubt, but to come to Christ just as you are, and to refer the doubt to him.

Often, when I call to see a troubled Christian, do you know what he is almost sure to say? "Oh, sir, I do not feel this—and I do fear that—and I cannot help thinking the other!" That great I is the root of all our sorrows, what I feel, or what I do not feel; that is enough to make anyone miserable. It is a wise plan to say to such a one, "Oh, yes! I know that all you say about yourself is only too true; but, now, let me hear what you have to say about Christ. For the next twenty-four hours at least, leave off thinking about yourself, and think only of Christ." O my dear friends, what a change would come over our spirits if we were all to act thus! For, when we have done with self, and cast all our care upon Christ, there remains no reason for us to care, or trouble, or fret.

David's other remedy for his soul, when it was cast down within him, was the grateful remembrance of the past when, by the Lord's tender mercies, it was lifted up: "therefore will I remember you from the land of Jordan and of Hermon, from Mount Mizar." Look up your old diary; many of you have gray hairs, so your notebooks go back a long way. Let us read one or two of the entries. Why, here is a bright page! Though the one preceding it is black, and full of sorrow, this page is bright with joy, and jubilant with song. Do you think that he is not standing by your side now? If there is a loud thundering, and if there is a thick darkness, will he leave you? Surely these reflections upon what you have experienced in the past should lead you to trust in Christ for the present. God forbid that we should ever think that he was so cruel as to enlighten, and comfort, and cheer, and help us so long, and then leave us at last to sink and to perish!

You, who have been at the foot of the cross, are afraid that you will be cast away at the last! You have known the sweetness of Jesus's love, yet you are cast down! He has kissed you with the kisses of his lips, his left hand has been under your head, and his right hand has embraced you, yet you think he will leave you at last in trouble to sink! You have been in his banqueting house, and you have had such food as angels never tasted, yet you dream that you shall be cast into hell! Shame upon you! Pluck off those robes of mourning, lay aside that sackcloth and those ashes, down from the willows snatch your harps, and let us together sing praises unto him whose love, and power, and faithfulness, and goodness, shall ever be the same.

Day 11
Jesus Wept

Jesus wept.
John 11:35

His humanity was our humanity to the full, although without sin. Sin is not essential to humanity: it is a disease of nature; it is not a feature found in humanity as it came from the Creator's hand. The Man of men, in whom all true humanity is found in perfection, is Christ Jesus.

The fact that Jesus wept is a clear proof of this. He wept for he had human friendships. Friendship is natural to man. Scarcely is he a man who never had a friend to love. Men in going through the world make many acquaintances, but out of these they have few special objects of esteem, whom they call friends. If they think to have many friends, they are, probably, misusing the name. All wise and good men have about them choice spirits, with whom their intercourse is more free, and in whom their trust is more confident than in all others. Jesus delighted to find retirement in the quiet home at Bethany; and we read that "Jesus loved Martha and her sister and Lazarus" (John 11:5). Alas, my brethren! every friendship opens a fresh door for grief; for friends are no more immortal than ourselves. "Jesus wept" at the grave of his friend just as you and I have done and must needs do again. Behold your Lord, like David weeping for his Jonathan (2 Samuel 1:17), and see how human he is in his friendships.

"Jesus wept," for he was truly human in his sympathies. He did not merely walk about among us, and look like a man, but at a thousand points he came into contact with us. Jesus was always in touch with sorrow; happy are they that are in touch with him! Our Lord saw Mary and Martha weeping, and the Jews weeping that were with her, and he caught the contagion of their grief: "Jesus wept." His sympathies were with sorrowing ones, and for this reason, among others, he was himself "a man of sorrows and acquainted with grief" (Isaiah 53:3). He loved first his Father in heaven, whose glory was his main object; but he loved intensely his chosen, and his sympathy with them knew no bounds. "In all their affliction he was afflicted" (Isaiah 63:9). Jesus was far more tender towards humanity than any other man has ever been. He was the great Philanthropist. Alas! Man is often the cruelest foe of man. None more unkind to man than men. Not the elements in their fury, nor wild beasts in their rage, nor diseases in their terror, have made such havoc among men as men drunk with the war spirit. When has there been such cruel hate on the part of the most savage monster towards man as has raged in the hearts of bloodthirsty warriors? To this hate our Lord was a perfect stranger. There was no flint in his heart. He was love, and only love; and through his love he descended into the depths of grief with the beloved ones whose lot was sorrowful; and he carried out to the full that sacred precept, "Weep with those who weep" (Romans 12:15). Jesus was no unsuffering seraph, no cherub incapable of grief, but he was bone of our bone, and flesh of our flesh; and therefore "Jesus wept."

He was a man, dear friends, for he was stirred with human emotion. Every emotion that ever thrilled through your bosom, so far as it is not sinful, has had its like in the bosom of the Lord Jesus Christ. He could be angry: we read in one place that "he looked round about on them with anger" (Mark 3:5). He could be compassionate; when was he not so? He could be moved with compassion for a fainting crowd, or with scorn of a crafty ruler. Did he not speak with great indignation of the scribes and Pharisees? Yet, was he not tender as a nurse with a child, when cheering the penitent? He would not break the bruised reed, nor quench the smoking flax (Isaiah 42:3); yet he uttered faithful warnings and made terrible exposures of hypocrisy. Our Savior, at the moment described in our text, felt indignation, pity, love, desire, and other emotions. He who is all bowels of tenderness, was stirred from head to foot. He was troubled, and he troubled himself. As when water is shaken in a vial, so was his whole nature shaken with a mighty emotion, as he stood at the grave of Lazarus, confronting death and him that hath the power of it. Our Lord proved himself a man when it was said that "Jesus wept."

See now the real sympathy of Christ with his people, for herein is comfort. If we fled to him for refuge, and found that he had known no grief, and consequently could not understand us, it would be killing to a broken heart. A Jesus who never wept could never wipe away my tears. That were a grief I could not bear, if he could not have fellowship with me, and could not understand my woe.

Beloved, think how bravely our Lord endured; herein is confidence. Tears did not drown the Savior's hope in God. He lived. He triumphed notwithstanding all his sorrow; and because he lives, we shall live also. He says, "Be of good cheer; I have overcome the world" (John 16:33 KJV). Though our hero had to weep in the fight, yet he was not beaten. He came, he wept, he conquered. You and I take losses and crosses with Jesus, we share the tears of his eyes, and we shall share the diamonds of his crown. Wear the thorn crown here, and you shall wear the crown of glory hereafter.

Day 12

Members of Christ

We are members of his body.
Ephesians 5:30

Paul here speaks only of true believers. Men who are quickened by divine grace and made alive unto God. Of them, he says, not by way of romance, nor of poetical exaggeration, but as an undisputed matter of fact, "We are members of his body, of his flesh, and of his bones." That there is a true union between Christ and his people is no fiction or dream of a heated imagination. Sin separated us from God, and in undoing what sin has done, Christ joins us to himself in a union more real than any other in the whole world.

This union is very near, and very dear, and very complete. We are so near to Christ, that we cannot be nearer; for we are one with him. We are so dear to Christ, that we cannot be dearer. Consider how close and tender is the tie when it is true that Christ loved us and gave himself for us. It is a union more intimate than any other which exists among men; for "Greater love has no one than this, that someone lay down his life for his friends" (John 15:13). We were his enemies when Christ died for us, that he might save us, and make us so one with himself, that from him our life should be drawn, and that in him our life should be hid. It is, then, a very near and dear union which Christ has established between himself and his redeemed; and this union could not be more complete than it is.

It is, also, a most wonderful union. The more you think of it, the more you will be astonished, and stand in sacred awe before such a marvel of grace.

O sacred union, firm and strong,
How great the grace, how sweet the song,
That worms of earth should ever be
One with Incarnate Deity!

But so it is. Even the incarnation of Christ is not more wonderful than his living union with his people. It is a thing to be considered often; it is the wonder of the skies; and is chief among those things which "the angels long to look into" (1 Peter 1:12). On the surface of this truth you may not see much; but the longer you gaze, and the more the Holy Spirit assists you in your meditation, the more you will see in this wonderful sea of glass mingled with fire. My soul exults in the doctrine that Christ and his people are everlastingly one.

This is a very cheering doctrine. He that understands it has an ocean of music in his soul. He that can really grasp and feed upon it will often sit in the heavenly places with his Lord and anticipate the day when he shall be with him, and shall be like him. Even now, since we are one with him, there is no distance between us, we are nearer to him than anything else can ever be. The very idea of union makes us forget all distance: indeed distance is altogether annihilated. Love joins us so closely with Christ, that he becomes more to us than our very selves; and though now we see him not, yet believing, we rejoice with joy unspeakable and full of glory.

Between the head and the members there is union of feeling. If the head aches, you feel it all over, you are altogether ill; and if your finger aches, your head does not feel well. There is such a sympathy between all parts of the body that, "if one member suffers, all suffer together; if one member is honored, all rejoice together. Now you are the body of Christ and individually members of it" (1 Corinthians 12:26–27). Christ is our Head, and the Head specially suffers with the members. I do not know whether it is always so clear that one hand suffers with another hand, as it is clear that the head suffers with either hand. So is it with the church. It may not always be clear that all the members sympathize with each other, but it is always clear that Christ sympathizes with each one of his people.

There is a quicker way, somehow, from the head to the hand, than there is from one hand to the other, and there is a keener sympathy between Christ and his people than there often is between one of his servants and another. It is written concerning his people that "In all their affliction he was afflicted" (Isaiah 63:9). In all your sorrows, child of God, your heavenly Head feels the pain!

Day 13
Sufferings to Be Expected

For as we share abundantly in Christ's sufferings,
so through Christ we share abundantly in comfort too.
2 Corinthians 1:5

Why must the Christian expect trouble? Why must he expect the sufferings of Christ to abound in him? Stand here a moment, my brother, and I will show you four reasons why you must endure trial. First look upward, then look downward, then look around you, and then look within yourself, and you will see four reasons why the sufferings of Christ should abound in you.

Look upward. Do you see your heavenly Father, a pure and holy being, spotless, just, and perfect? Do you know that you are one day to be like him? Do you think you will easily come to be conformed to his image? Will you not require much furnace work, much grinding in the mill of trouble, much breaking with the pestle in the mortar of affliction, much being broken under the wheels of agony? Do you think it will be an easy thing for your heart to become as pure as God is? Do you think you can so soon get rid of your corruptions, and become perfect, even as your Father which is in heaven is perfect?

Lift up your eye again; do you discern those bright spirits clad in white, purer than alabaster, more chaste, more fair than Parian marble? Behold them as they stand in glory. Ask them whence their victory came. Some of them will tell you—they swam through seas of blood. Behold the sears of honor on their brows; see, some of them lift up their hands and tell you they were once consumed in fire; while others were slain by the sword, rent in pieces by wild beasts, were destitute, afflicted, tormented. O you noble army of martyrs, you glorious hosts of the living God. Must you swim through seas of blood, and shall I hope to ride to heaven wrapped in furs and ermine? Did you endure suffering, and shall I be hampered with the luxuries of this world? Did you fight and then reign, and must I reign without a battle? Oh, no. By God's help I will expect that as he suffered so must I, and as through much tribulation you entered the kingdom of heaven, so shall I.

Next, Christian, turn your eyes downward. Do you know what foes you have beneath your feet? There is hell and its lions against you. You were once a servant of Satan, and no king will willingly lose his subjects. Do you think that Satan is pleased with you? Why, have you changed your country. You were once a liege servant of Apollyon, but now you have become a good soldier of Jesus Christ; and do you think the devil is pleased with you? Ah! no. He will always be at you, for your enemy, "prowls around like a roaring lion, seeking someone to devour" (1 Peter 5:8). Expect trouble therefore, Christian, when you look beneath you.

Then, man of God, look around you. Do not be asleep. Open your eyes, and look around you. Where are you? Is that man a friend next to you? No; you are in an enemy's country. This is a wicked world. Half the people, I suppose, profess to be irreligious and those who profess to be pious, often are not. "Cursed is the man who trusts in man and makes flesh his strength"—"Blessed is the man that trusts in the Lord, whose trust is the Lord" (Jeremiah 17:5, 7)—As for "men of low degree," they are vanity; the voice of the crowd is not worth having; and as for "men of high degree," they are a lie (Psalm 62:9 KJV), which is worse still. The world is not to be trusted in, not to be relied upon. The true Christian treads it beneath his feet, with "all that earth calls good or great." Look around you my brother; you will see some good hearts, strong and valiant, you will see some true souls, sincere and honest, you will see some faithful lovers of Christ; but I tell you, O child of light, that where you meet one sincere man, you will meet twenty hypocrites, where you will find one that will lead you to heaven, you will find a score who would push you to hell. You are in a land of enemies, not of friends. Never believe the world is good for much. Many people have burned their fingers by taking hold of it. You are in an enemy's country, man: therefore, expect trouble; expect that you shall be estranged from those that love you; be assured that, since you are in the land of the foe, you shall find foemen everywhere.

But then, look within you. There is a little world in here, which is quite enough to give us trouble. Sin is there—original sin and corruption; and, what is more, self is still within. Ah! if you had no devil to tempt you, you would tempt yourself; if there were no enemies to fight you, yourself would be your worst foe; if there were no world, still yourself would be bad enough; for "the heart is deceitful above all things, and desperately sick" (Jeremiah 17:9). Look within you, believer, know that you bear a cancer in your very vitals; that you carry within you a bombshell, ready to burst at the slightest spark of temptation, know that you have inside your heart an evil thing, a coiled-up viper, ready to sting you and bring you into trouble, and pain, and misery unutterable.

Now do you see, brother Christian? No hope to escape trouble is there. What shall we do then? There is no chance for us. We must bear suffering and affliction; therefore, let us endure it cheerfully. Some of us are the officers in God's regiments, and we are the mark of all the riflemen of the enemy. Standing forward, we have to bear all the shots. What a mercy it is that not one of God's officers ever fall in battle! God always keeps them. When the arrows fly fast, the shield of faith catches them all; and when the enemy is most angry, God is most pleased. So, for aught we care, the world may go on, the devil may revile, flesh may rise, "for we are more than conquerors through him who loved us" (Romans 8:37). Therefore, all honor be unto God alone.

Day 14

A Sharp Knife for the Branches

Every branch in me that does not bear fruit he takes away,
and every branch that does bear fruit he prunes,
that it may bear more fruit.
John 15:2

Pruning is the lot of all the fruitful saints. You may escape it if you are not fruitful, but all the fruit-bearing saints must feel the knife. How does the Lord prune his people, then? It is generally said by affliction; I question if that could be proved as it stands; it needs explanation. It is generally thought that our trials and troubles purge us; I am not sure of that, they certainly are lost upon some. Our Lord tells us what it is that prunes us. "Now," says he, "ye are clean (or pruned) through the word which I have spoken unto you" (John 15:3 KJV). It is the word that prunes the Christian, it is the truth that purges him, the Scripture, made living and powerful by the Holy Spirit, effectually cleanses the Christian.

"What then does affliction do?" say you. Well, if I may say so, affliction is the handle of the knife; affliction is the grindstone that sharpens up the word; affliction is the dresser which removes our soft garments, and lays bare the diseased flesh, so that the surgeon's lancet may get at it; affliction makes us ready to feel the word, but the true pruner is the word in the hand of the Great Husbandman. Sometimes when you lay stretched upon the bed of sickness, you think more upon the word than you did before, that is one great thing. In the next place, you see more the applicability of that word to yourself. In the third place, the Holy Spirit makes you feel more, while you are thus laid aside, the force of the word than you did before. Ask that affliction may be sanctified, beloved, but always remember there is no more tendency in affliction in itself to sanctify us than there is in prosperity; in fact, the natural tendency of affliction is to make us rebel against God, which is quite opposite to sanctification. It is the word coming to us while in affliction that purges us; it is God the Holy Ghost laying home divine truth, and applying the blood of Jesus, and working in all his divine energy in the soul; it is this that prunes us, and affliction is only the handle of the knife, or what if I say the ladder which the gardener takes to reach the vine, so that he may prune it the better!

Now, it may be that some of us have been afflicted a great deal and have not been pruned. I know some people who have been very poor, I do not see that they are any better for it, and I know some others who have been very sick, and I have never heard that they have been improved. Alas! some people are of such a character, that if they were stricken till their whole head were sick, and their whole heart faint, they would not be benefited; if they were beaten till they were all bruises and putrid sores, they would still go on to rebel, for these things only provoke them to a greater hatred against the Most High. We must be pruned, but it must be by the word, through affliction.

Now, the object in this pruning is never condemnatory. God does not purge his children with a view to visit them penalty for sin; he chastises, but he cannot punish those for whom Jesus Christ has been already punished. You have no right to say, when a man is afflicted, that it is because he has done wrong; on the contrary, "every branch that does bear fruit he prunes." Just the branch that is good for something gets the pruning knife. Do not say of yourselves, or of other people, "That man must have been a great offender, or he would not have met with such a judgment." Nonsense! Who was a holier man than Job; but who was brought lower than he? Why, the fact is, it is because the Lord loves his people that he chastens them, not because of any anger that he has towards them. But learn, beloved, especially as you are under trial, not to see an angry God in your pains or your losses, or your crosses; but instead thereof, see a husbandman, who thinks you a branch whom he estimates at so great a rate, that he will take the trouble to prune you, which he would not do if he had not a kind consideration towards you.

The real reason is that more fruit may be produced; which I understand to mean more in quantity. A good man, who feels the power of the word pruning him of this and that superfluity, sets to work, in the power of the Holy Ghost, to do more for Jesus. Before he was afflicted, he did not know how to be patient. He learns it at last—a hard lesson. Before he was poor, he did not know how to be humble, but he learns that. Before the word came with power, he did not know how to pray with his fellows, or to speak to sinners, or lay himself out for usefulness; but the more he is pruned, the more he serves his Lord. More fruit in variety too, may be intended. One tree can only produce one kind of fruit usually, but the Lord's people can produce many, as we have already seen; and the more they are pruned, the more they will produce. There will be all kinds of fruits, both new and old, which they will lay up for their beloved. There will be more in quality, too. The man may not pray more, but he will pray more earnestly; he may not preach more sermons, but he will preach them more thoroughly from his heart, with a greater unction. It may be that he will not be more in communion with God as to time, but it will be a closer communion; he will throw himself more thoroughly into the divine element of communion and will become more hearty in all that he does.

This is the result of the pruning which our heavenly Father gives; and if such be the result, may the Lord keep on pruning, for what greater blessing can a man have than to produce much fruit for God?

Day 15

The Education of Sons of God

Although he was a son, he learned obedience
through what he suffered.
Hebrews 5:8

It is put as if this might have been a case where the rod of the household could have been spared. That there should be suffering for enemies, that there should be sorrow for rebels against God, is natural and proper; but one might have thought that he would have spared his own Son, and that, in his case, there would be no learning of obedience by the things which he suffered. But, according to the text, Sonship did not exempt the Lord Jesus Christ from suffering. I want you to notice that, in his case, the Sonship was very emphatic. It was a relationship which was enjoyed by him by nature. He was the Son of God before ever the worlds were made, before time began. We know not how it was, neither may we attempt to explain the doctrine of the eternal Filiation; but, assuredly, as long as there was a Father, there was a Son, and Jesus Christ has ever been "the Son of the Most High" (Luke 1:32).

Yet, though he was a Son, when he came and took upon himself our nature, and appeared on earth, he was not exempted from learning obedience by the things which he suffered. In person he was august; he was the Heir of all things, the King of all kings, the King's Son as well as King himself; and yet, notwithstanding the loftiness of his nature, and the unspeakable majesty of his rank, he "learned obedience through what he suffered." Though Jesus was a

Son, yet he learned obedience. As God, our Savior knew everything. As God, however, he did not obey. It was in his complex character as our Mediator that he learned to obey.

Perhaps some of you are asking, "But why cannot we obey without learning obedience?" The reason is because obedience has to be learned experimentally. If a man is to learn a trade thoroughly, he must be apprenticed to it. A soldier, sitting at home, and reading books, will not learn the deadly art of war. He must go to the barracks, and the camp, and the field of battle if he is to win victories, and become a veteran. The dry land sailor, who never went even in a boat, would not know much about navigation, study hard as he might; he must go to sea to be a sailor. So, obedience is a trade to which a man must be apprenticed until he has learned it, for it is not to be known in any other way. Even our blessed Lord could not have fully learned obedience by the observation in others of such an obedience as he had personally to render, for there was no one from whom he could thus learn.

"Why!" says somebody, "he might have learned obedience from the angels, who do God's commandments, hearkening unto the voice of his Word" (Psalm 103:20). Ah, but angels had never suffered! They have not bodies like ours, full of infirmities; and that kind of passive obedience, which our Savior had mainly to render, is not required of them. Angels could not be "obedient to the point of death, even death on the cross" (Philippians 2:8); so that our Lord Jesus could not see in them such an obedience as he had covenanted to render on behalf of his people, when he engaged to stand in their stead, and to keep the law which they could not keep. He could not learn obedience by observation; he must learn it by experience. What was to be done, what was to be suffered, he must learn by doing it, and suffering it.

It was in the doing of it that he became actually, personally, experimentally acquainted with what was meant by perfect obedience to the will of God; and he did it, brethren. He went right through with that lesson until he had learned obedience. He was getting near to the end of his great task when he said, "Not as I will, but as you will" (Matthew 26:39); but he had fully learned it when he said, "It is finished" (John 19:30). He had come to the last line of his lesson; he knew it thoroughly; he had learned obedience. He had to learn obedience in order that he might save us, for it was God's "righteous Servant" who was to "justify many" (Isaiah 53:11 KJV).

Why have you and I, dear friends, to learn obedience? Because there is no way of obtaining true happiness but by obedience. Sin always has sorrow at the tail of it. Happiness is obedience, and obedience is happiness. If we do the will of the Lord thoroughly, then are we delivered from all evil, and enter into the joy of our Lord. We have also to learn obedience because there could be no heaven without it. We hope to go on obeying our Lord forever and ever. Up yonder, in the heaven of glorified spirits, there is perfect obedience to the will of God; and you and I expect to go there, so we want to learn the music here until we know it and can join the choirs above without creating discord. We are going through our practice and rehearsals now. It takes a great deal of time and patience to teach even some Christian people obedience. Many of us are more like a weaning child, crying, fretting, rebelling. We have not laid all our wishes at Jesus's feet, and said to him, "Not my will, but yours be done." But it is essential that we should come to this point; we should not be fit for heaven if we did not, for all the spirits before the throne bow submissively to the will of God. They have neither wish nor desire apart from God's will; they have no wandering ambitions, no selfish aims; their every thought is brought into captivity to the will of God. Let us pray for this: "Your will be done on earth, as it is in heaven (Matthew 6:10); and let it be done in our hearts, good Lord, or else we shall never be fit to enter there."

Day 16

Suffering and Reigning with Jesus

if we endure, we will also reign with him;
if we deny him, he also will deny us;
2 Timothy 2:12

To suffer, is the common lot of all men. It is not possible for us to escape from it. We come into this world through the gate of suffering, and over death's door hangs the same escutcheon. We must suffer if we live, no matter in what style we spend our existence. To suffer is not peculiar to the Christian, neither does suffering necessarily bring with it any recompense of reward. The text implies most clearly that we must suffer with Christ in order to reign with him. The suffering which brings the reigning with Jesus, must be a suffering with Jesus.

There is a very current error among those poor people who are ignorant of true religion, that all poor and afflicted people will be rewarded for it in the next state. It is a work of grace in the heart and character, which shall decide the future, not poverty or wealth. Let intelligent persons combat this notion whenever they meet with it. Suffering here does not imply happiness hereafter. It is only a certain order of suffering to which a reward is promised, the suffering which comes to us from fellowship with the Lord Jesus, and conformity to his image.

Supposing a man to be in Christ, yet it does not even then follow that all his sufferings are sufferings with Christ, for it is essential that he be called by God to suffer. If a good man were, out of mistaken views of mortification and self-denial, to mutilate his body, or to flog his flesh as many a sincere enthusiast has done, I might admire the man's fortitude, but I should not allow for an instant that he was suffering with Christ. Who called men to such austerities? Certainly not the God of love. If, therefore, they torture themselves at the command of their own fancies, fancy must reward them, for God will not.

Again, in troubles which come upon us as the result of sin, we must not think we are suffering with Christ. If you do wrong and suffer for it, what thanks have you (1 Peter 2:20)? Go behind the door and weep for your sin, but come not forth in public to claim a reward. Many a hypocrite, when he has had his deserts, and has been called by his proper name, has cried out, "Ah! I am persecuted." It is not an infallible sign of excellence to be in bad repute among men. Who feels any esteem for a cold-blooded murderer? Does not every man reprobate the offender? Is he, therefore, a Christian because he is spoken against, and his name cast out as evil? Assuredly not; he is heartless villain and nothing more.

Suffering such as God accepts and rewards for Christ's sake, must have God's glory as its end. If I suffer that, I may earn a name, or win applause among men; if I venture into trial merely that I may be respected for it, I shall get my reward; but it will be the reward of the Pharisee, and not the crown of the sincere servant of the Lord Jesus. I must mind, too, that love to Christ, and love to his elect, is ever the mainspring of all my patience; remembering the apostle's words, "if I deliver up my body to be burned, but have not love, I gain nothing" (I Corinthians 13:3). If I suffer in bravado, filled with proud defiance of my fellow-men; if I love the dignity of singularity, and out of dogged obstinacy hold to an opinion, not because it is right—and I love God too well to deny his truth—but because I choose to think as I like, then I suffer not with Jesus. If there be no love to God in my soul; if I do not endure all things for the elect's sake (2 Timothy 2:10), I may bear many a cuff and buffeting, but I miss the fellowship of the Spirit, and have no recompense.

If in your service for Christ, you are enabled so to sacrifice yourself, that you bear upon yourself inconvenience and pain, labor and loss, then I think you are suffering with Christ. The missionary who tempts the stormy deep—the herald of the cross who penetrates into unknown regions among savage men—the colporteur[1] toiling up the mountain-side—the teacher going wearily to the class—the village preacher walking many toilsome miles—the minister starving on a miserable pittance—the evangelist content to break down in health—all these and their like, suffer with Christ. We are all too much occupied with taking care of ourselves; we shun the difficulties of excessive labor. And frequently behind the entrenchments of taking care of our constitution, we do not half as much as we ought. A minister of God is bound to spurn the suggestions of ignoble ease, it is his calling to labor; and if he destroys his constitution, I for one, only thank God that he permits us the high privilege of so making ourselves living sacrifices.

Brethren, if you are thus called to suffer for Christ, will you quarrel with me if I say, in adding all up, what a very little

1. Colporteurs were traveling salesmen common in the nineteenth century who specialized in circulating Bibles and religious materials.

it is compared with reigning with Jesus! "For our light affliction, which is but for a moment, is working for us a far more exceeding and eternal weight of glory" (2 Corinthians 4:17 NKJV). When I contrast our sufferings of today with those of the reign of Mary, or the persecutions of the Albigenses[2] on the mountains, or the sufferings of Christians in Pagan Rome, why ours are scarcely a pin's prick! And yet what is the reward? We shall reign with Christ. There is no comparison between the service and the reward. Therefore it is all of grace. We do but little, and suffer but little—and even that little grace gives us—and yet the Lord grants us "a far more exceeding and eternal weight of glory." We are not merely to sit with Christ, but we are to reign with Christ. All that the pomp imperial of his kingship means; all that the treasure of his wide dominions can yield; all that the majesty of his everlasting power can bestow—all this is to belong to you, given to you of his rich, free grace, as the sweet reward of having suffered for a little time with him.

2. The Albigenses (or Albigensians) were a dissenting religious sect, critical of the Roman Catholic Church, that arose between the eleventh and fourteenth century in southern France.

Day 17
Counting the Cost

If anyone comes to me and does not hate his own father and mother and wife and children and brothers and sisters, yes, and even his own life, he cannot be my disciple. Whoever does not bear his own cross and come after me cannot be my disciple. For which of you, desiring to build a tower, does not first sit down and count the cost, whether he has enough to complete it?
Luke 14:26–28

You may be sure that the cost must be great, since our Lord compares it to the building of a tower. The word here used for "tower" has often been employed to signify a turreted house, a villa, or country mansion. "Which of you," says he to the people, "intending to build for himself a mansion in which to reside at your ease would not first of all count the cost?" The building is to be a costly one. That it would cost a considerable sum is clear from the Savior's saying that the wise man sits down and counts the cost. He does not merely stand up and pass his hand over his brow, and say, "This tower will cost me so many hundred pounds," but it is to be an elaborate construction, an almost palatial edifice, and therefore he sits down, like a merchant at his desk, and thoughtfully considers the undertaking; he consults the architect and the mason, and calculates what will be the expense of the outer walls, what of the roof, what of the interior fittings, and the like, and he does not make a rough guess, but counts the cost as men count their gold. It is evidently a matter of consequence with him, and so is true religion—it is no trifle, but an all-important business.

What, then, is the expense? What is the cost of building this tower? The answer is given by our Savior, not by me. I should not have dared to invent such tests as he has ordained; it is for me to be the echo of his voice and no more. What does he say? Why, first, that if you would be his and have his salvation, you must love him beyond every other person in this world. Is not that the meaning of this expression, "If anyone comes to me and does not hate his father and mother and wife and children and brothers and sisters"? I am afraid that many professors are not prepared for this. They would be Christians if their family would approve, but they must consult their brother, father, or wife. They would make a stand against worldly pleasures if others would, but they cannot bear to appear singular, or to oppose the views of relatives.

Mark you, you will best prove your love to your relatives by being decided for the right, since you will be the more likely to win their souls. Love them too much to indulge the wrong in them; love them so truly that you hate that in them which would injure you and ruin them. You must be prepared to suffer from those who are bound to you by the dearest ties; sin must not be tolerated whatever may happen. We cannot yield in the point of sin, our determination is invincible; come hate or come love, we must follow Christ.

The next item of cost is this—self must be hated. It means this: that wherein my own pleasure, or my own gain, or my own repute, or even my own life shall come in the way of Christ's glory, I am so little to make any account of myself, that I must even hate myself if self shall stand in the way of Christ. I am to look upon father, mother, brother, sister, and myself also, as foes, so far as they are opposed to the Lord Jesus and his holy will. I am to love them and desire their good as I also desire good for myself, but I am not to desire any good for them or for myself at the cost of sinning, and robbing the Lord Jesus of his glory. As for myself, if I see anything in myself opposed to Jesus I must do away with it. I must mortify the flesh with its affections and lusts, denying myself anything and everything which would grieve the Savior, or would prevent my realizing perfect conformity to him.

Next, the Savior goes on to say that if we would follow him we must bear our cross: "Whoever does not bear his own cross and come after me cannot be my disciple." Sometimes that cross comes in the shape of confessing our faith before gainsayers. "Ah," says the timid heart, "if I do so I shall have all my friends against me." Take up your cross! it is a part of the cost of true discipleship. "I shall scarcely be able to bear myself in the house if I avow my religion." Take up your cross! my brother, or you cannot be Christ's disciple. "Well, but it will involve a change even in my daily life." Make the change, my brother, or you cannot be the Lord's disciple. "But I know there is one very dear whom I have looked upon as likely to be my future companion, and he will leave me if I forsake the ways of the world." Then, heavy as the loss may be, let him go, if it be so that you cannot follow Christ and unite with him; for Jesus you must follow, or be lost forever. If any man love the world the love of the Father is not in him, and he who has the smile of the ungodly must look for the frown of God.

Last of all, we must make an unreserved surrender of all to Jesus. Listen to these words: "So therefore, any one of you who does not renounce all that he has cannot be my disciple" (Luke 14:33). It may yet come to this, that persecution may arise, and you may have actually to give up all. You must be prepared for the event. You may not have to give up anything, but the surrender must be just as real in your heart as if it had to be carried out in act and deed.

Is there any getting to heaven without this cost? No. But may we not be Christians without these sacrifices? You may be counterfeits, you may be hypocrites, you may be brethren of Judas, but you cannot be real Christians. This cost is unavoidable, it cannot be bated one solitary mite. God grant you may be enabled to submit to it.

Day 18

A Wonderful Transformation

Truly, truly, I say to you, you will weep and lament,
but the world will rejoice. You will be sorrowful,
but your sorrow will turn into joy.
John 16:20

In speaking those comforting words to his disciples, our Savior made use of this memorable sentence, "Your sorrow will turn into joy." As I read the whole passage, I pondered over those words, and tried to find out their meaning. Perhaps you think, as you glance at them, that they mean that the man who was sorrowful would be joyous. That is part of their meaning, but they mean a great deal more than that. They mean, literally and actually, your sorrow itself shall be turned into joy—not the sorrow to be taken away, and joy to be put in its place, but the very sorrow, which now grieves you, shall be turned into joy. This is a very wonderful transformation; and only the God who works great marvels could possibly accomplish it—could, somehow, not only take away the bitterness, and give sweetness in its place, but turn the bitterness itself into sweetness.

Our sorrows, dear friends, are turned into joy in many different ways. For instance, there are some of us, who are such naughty children, that we never seem to come close to our Heavenly Father unless some sorrow drives us to him. We ought to be more with him in days of sunshine, if it were possible, than in days of storm, but it is not always so. It is said that there are some dogs which, the more you whip them, the more they love you. I should not like to try that plan even on a dog; but I fear that some of us are very like dogs, in that respect, if the saying is true. When we have a great trouble, we seem to wake up and say, "Lord, we forgot you when all was going smoothly; we wandered from you then, but now we must come back to you." And there is a special softness of heart, and mellowness of spirit, which we often get through being tried and troubled; and when that is the case, you and I have great cause to rejoice in our sorrows, if they draw us nearer to God, and bring us to a clear and more careful walk with him. If they draw us away from worldliness, and self-sufficiency, and self-complacency, our sorrows, if we are wise men and women, will be immediately turned into joy.

Again, there is no doubt that, to many, sorrow is a great means of opening the eyes to the preciousness of the promises of God. I believe that there are some of God's promises, of which we shall never get to know the meaning until we have been placed in the circumstances for which those promises were written. Certain objects in nature can only be seen from certain points of view, and there are precious things in the covenant of grace that can only be perceived from the deep places of trouble. Well, then, if your trouble brings you into a position where you can understand more of the lovingkindness of the Lord, you may be very thankful that you were ever put there, and may thus find your sorrow turned into joy.

Again, sorrow often gives us further fellowship with Christ. There are times when we can say, "Now, Lord, we can sympathize with you better than we ever did before, for we have felt somewhat as you did in your agony here below." We have sometimes felt as though that prophecy had been fulfilled to us, "You will indeed drink My cup, and be baptized with the baptism that I am baptized with" (Matthew 20:23 NKJV). For instance, if friends forsake you, you can say, "Now, Lord, I know a little better what your feeling was when Judas so basely betrayed you." You cannot so fully comprehend the griefs of Christ unless, in your humble measure, you have to pass through a somewhat similar experience; but when you perceive that you can sympathize more with Christ because of your own sorrow, then, for certain, your sorrow is turned into joy.

Sorrow also gives us fellowship with our Lord in another way—when we feel as if Christ and we had become partners in one trouble. Here is a cross, and I have to carry one end of it; but I look round, and see that my Lord is carrying the heavier end of it, and then it is a very sweet sorrow to carry the cross in partnership with Christ. Rutherford says, in one of his letters, "When Christ's dear child is carrying a burden, it often happens that Christ says, 'Halves, my love,' and carries the half of it for him." It is indeed sweet when it is so. Our motto must be, "Anywhere with Jesus, nowhere without Jesus." Where Jesus is, our sorrow is turned into joy.

I must not fail to remind you that there is a time coming when "the sorrows of death" (Psalm 18:4 KJV) will get hold upon us, and I want you, brethren and sisters, to understand that, when the Lord shall come, we shall not escape the sorrow of dying, but it will be turned into joy. Some of you may be dreading death, for there is still a measure of unbelief remaining in you; but, in your case also, death, will be swallowed up in victory. Some of you are very poor, and others of you are very much tried and troubled in many ways; but, my dear friends, when you and I get up there—and we shall do so before long—I think you will have the best of it. If there is any truth in that line—"The deeper their sorrows, the louder they'll sing"—the more sorrows you have had, the more will you sing. Nobody enjoys wealth like a man who has been poor. Nobody enjoys health like a man who has been sick. I think that the pleasantest days I ever spend are them that follow a long illness, when I at last begin to creep out of doors, and drink in the sweet fresh air again. And, oh, what joy it will be to you, poor ones, and you, sick ones, and you, tried ones, to get into the land where all is plentiful, where all is peaceful, where all is gladsome, where all is holy!

Day 19
For the Troubled

Your wrath lies heavy upon me,
and you overwhelm me with all your waves.
Psalm 88:7

Saints do well to trace all their trials to their God. Heman did so in the text: "Your wrath lies heavy upon me, and you overwhelm me with all your waves." He traces all his adversity to the Lord his God. It is God's wrath, they are God's waves that afflict him, and God makes them afflict him. Child of God, never forget this; all that you are suffering of any sort, or kind, comes to you from the divine hand. Truly, you say, "my affliction arises from wicked men," yet remember that there is a predestination which, without soiling the fingers of the Infinitely Holy, nevertheless rules the motions of evil men as well as of holy angels.

It were a dreary thing for us if there were no appointments of God's providence which concerned the ungodly; then the great mass of mankind would be entirely left to chance, and the godly might be crushed by them without hope. The Lord, without interfering with the freedom of their wills, rules and overrules, so that the ungodly are as a rod in his hand, with which he wisely scourges his children. Perhaps you will say that your trials have arisen not from the sins of others, but from your own sin. Even then I would have you penitently trace them still to God. What though the trouble spring out of the sin, yet it is God that has appointed the sorrow to follow the transgression, to act as a remedial agency for your spirit. Look not at the second cause, or, looking at it with deep regret, turn your eye chiefly to your heavenly Father.

The more we get away from intermediate agents the better, for when we reach to God, grace will make submission easy. When we know "it is the Lord," we readily cry, "let him do what seems him good" (1 Samuel 3:18). As long as I trace my pain to accident, my bereavement to mistake, my loss to another's wrong, my discomfort to an enemy, and so on, I am of the earth, and shall break my teeth with gravel stones; but when I rise to my God and see his hand at work, I grow calm, I have not a word of repining, "I do not open my mouth, for it is you who have done it" (Psalm 39:9). David preferred to fall into the hands of God (2 Samuel 24:14), and every believer knows that he feels safest and happiest when he recognizes that he is even yet in the divine hands. Caviling with man is poor work, but pleading with God brings help and comfort. "Cast your burden on the LORD" (Psalm 55:22) is a precept which it will be easy to practice when you see that the burden came originally from God.

But now, afflicted children of God do well to have a keen eye to the wrath that mingles with their troubles. "Your wrath lies heavy upon me." There is Heman's first point. He does not mention the waves of affliction till he has first spoken of the wrath. We should labor to discover what the Lord means by smiting us; what he purposes by the chastisement, and how far we can answer that purpose. We must use a keen eye clearly to distinguish things. There is an anger and an anger, a wrath and a wrath.

God is never angry with his children in one sense, but he is in another. As men, we have all of us disobeyed the laws of God, and God stands in relationship to all of us as a judge. As a judge, he must execute upon us the penalties of his law, and he must, from the necessity of his nature, be angry with us for having broken that law. That concerns all the human race. But the moment a man believes in the Lord Jesus Christ his offenses are his offenses no longer; they are laid upon Christ Jesus, the substitute, and the anger goes with the sin. The anger of God towards the sins of believers has spent itself upon Christ. Christ has been punished in their stead; the punishment due to their sin has been borne by Jesus Christ. God forbid that the Judge of all the earth should ever be unjust; it would not be just for God to punish a believer for a sin which has been already laid upon Jesus Christ.

Now, then, the Christian man takes up another position; he is adopted into the family of God: he has become God's child. He is under the law of God's house. There is in every house an economy, a law by which the children and servants are ruled. If the child of God breaks the law of the house, the Father will visit his offense with fatherly discipline—a very different kind of visitation from that of a judge. The father loves the child while he disciplines, and disciplines for that very reason (Hebrews 12:5–6). If it were not his child, he would probably take no notice of fault, but because it is his own boy who has spoken an untruth or committed an act of disobedience he feels he must chastise him because he loves him. This needs no further explanation.

There is a righteous anger in God's heart towards guilty impenitent men. He feels none of that towards his people. He is their father, and if they transgress, he will visit them with discipline, not as a legal punishment, since Christ has borne all that, but as a gentle paternal chastisement, that they may see their folly and repent of it; and that awakened by his tender hand, they may turn unto their Father and amend their ways. Now, child of God, if you are suffering today in any way whatever, whether from the ills of poverty or bodily sickness, or depression of spirits, recollect there is not a drop of the judicial anger of God in it all. You are not being punished for your sins as a judge punishes a culprit; never believe such false doctrine, it is clean contrary to the truth as it is in Jesus. Gospel doctrine tells us that our sins were numbered on the Great Scapegoat's head of old, and carried away once for all, never to be charged against us again (Leviticus 16:10).

Day 20

A Woman Troubled in Spirit

But Hannah answered, "No, my lord, I am a woman troubled in spirit. I have drunk neither wine nor strong drink, but I have been pouring out my soul before the Lord."
1 Samuel 1:15

Much that is precious may come out of a troubled spirit: it is not only to be found with it, but may even grow out of it.

Observe, first, that through her troubled spirit Hannah had learned to pray. I will not say but what she prayed before this great sorrow struck her, but this I know, she prayed with more intensity than before when she heard her rival talk so exceeding proudly and saw herself to be utterly despised. Oh! brothers and sisters, if you have a secret grief, learn where to carry it, and delay not to take it there. Learn from Hannah. Her appeal was to the Lord. She poured not out the secret of her soul into mortal ear, but spread her grief before God in his own house, and in his own appointed manner. She was in bitterness of soul and prayed to the Lord. Bitterness of soul should always be thus sweetened. Many are in bitterness of soul, but they do not pray, and therefore the taste of the wormwood remains. O that they were wise, and looked upon their sorrows as the divine call for prayer, the cloud which brings a shower of supplication! Our troubles should be steeds upon which we ride to God; rough winds which hurry our ship into the haven of all—prayer. When the heart is merry we may sing psalms, but concerning the afflicted, it is written, "Let him pray" (James 5:13). Thus, bitterness of spirit may be an index of our need of prayer, and an incentive to that holy exercise.

O daughter of sorrow, if in your darkened chamber you learn the art of prevailing with the Well-Beloved, bright-eyed maidens, down whose cheeks no tears have ever rushed, may well envy you, for to be proficient in the art and mystery of prayer is to be as a prince with God. May God grant that if we are of a troubled spirit, we may in the same proportion be of a prayerful spirit; and we need scarcely desire a change.

In the next place, Hannah had learned self-denial. This is clear, since the very prayer by which she hoped to escape out of her great grief was a self-denying one. She desired a son, that her reproach might be removed; but if her eyes might be blessed with such a sight, she would cheerfully resign her darling to be the Lord's as long as he lived. Mothers wish to keep their children about them. It is natural that they should wish to see them often. But Hannah, when most eager for a man-child, asking but for one, and that one as the special gift of God, yet does not seek him for herself, but for her God. She has it on her heart that, as soon as she has weaned him, she will take him up to the house of God and leave him there, as a dedicated child whom she can only see at certain festivals. Read her own words: "O Lord of hosts, if you will indeed look on the affliction of your servant and remember me and not forget your servant, but will give to your servant a son, then I will give him to the Lord all the days of his life, and no razor shall touch his head" (1 Samuel 1:11). Her heart longs not to see her boy at home, his father's daily pride, and her own hourly solace, but to see him serving as a Levite in the house of the Lord. She thus proved that she had learned self-denial.

Brethren and sisters, this is one of our hardest lessons: to learn to give up what we most prize at the command of God, and to do so cheerfully. This is real self-denial, when we ourselves make the proposition and offer the sacrifice freely, as she did. To desire a blessing that we may have the opportunity of parting with it, this is self-conquest: have we reached it? O you of a troubled spirit, if you have learned to crucify the flesh, if you have learned to keep under the body, if you have learned to cast all your desires and wills at his feet, you have gained what a thousand times repays you for all the losses and crosses you have suffered. Personally, I bless God for joy. I think I could sometimes do with a little more of it! But I fear, when I take stock of my whole life, that I have very seldom made any real growth in grace except as the result of being digged about and dunged by the stern husbandry of pain. My leaf is greenest in showery weather; my fruit is sweetest when it has been frosted by a winter's night.

Another precious thing had come to this woman, and that was, she had learned faith. She had become proficient in believing promises. It is very beautiful to note how at one moment she was in bitterness, but as soon as Eli had said, "Go in peace; and the God of Israel grant your petition that you have made of him." The woman "went her way and ate, and her face was no longer sad" (1 Samuel 1:17–18). She had not yet obtained the blessing, but she was persuaded of the promise and embraced it, after that Christly fashion which our Lord taught us when he said, " Therefore I tell you, whatever you ask in prayer, believe that you have received it, and it will be yours" (Mark 11:24); she wiped her tears, and smoothed the wrinkles from her brow, knowing that she was heard. By faith she held a man-child in her arms and presented it to the Lord. This is no small virtue to attain. When a troubled spirit has learned to believe God, to roll its burden upon him, and bravely to expect succor and help from him, it has learned by its losses how to make its best gains—by its griefs how to unfold its richest joys. Hannah is one of the honored band who through faith "obtained promises" (Hebrews 11:33). Therefore, O you who are of a troubled spirit, there is no reason why you should not also be of a believing spirit, even as she was.

Day 21

The Best Burden for Young Shoulders

It is good for a man that he bear
the yoke in his youth.
Lamentations 3:27

A good number of you have been lately converted, and to you, I speak most earnestly. It will be for your good as long as ever you live to render to Jesus complete obedience at the very first. Some Christians seem to me to start to Canaan all in a muddle; they do not begin their pilgrimage in the right pilgrim fashion. Every young Christian when he is converted should take time to consider, and should say to himself, "What am I to do? What is the duty of a Christian?" He should also devoutly say to the Lord Jesus, "Lord, show me what you would have me to do," and wait upon the Holy Ghost for guidance.

Now, if you young people begin conscientiously studying the word, and desiring in everything to put your feet down where Christ put his feet, I am sure it will be good for you. You will grow up to be healthy Christians and men of no ordinary stature. But if you do not begin with searching the Word, but take your religion at second-hand from other people, and do what you see other people do, without searching, why, you will lack that noble independence of mind and courage of spirit, and, at the same time, that complete submission to Christ, which make up the main elements of a noble-minded Christian.

It is good for young converts also to bear the yoke by beginning to serve Jesus Christ early. I like to see the mother when she brings her little one to the house of God put the penny into its hand and teach it early to contribute to the cause of Christ; and when people are converted there is nothing like their having something to do very soon. Not that they are to attempt to do the major things which belong to the more advanced and instructed; for, concerning some of these, we should apply the rule, "he must not be a recent convert, or he may become puffed up with conceit and he fall into the condemnation of the devil" (1 Timothy 3:6). But there is work for every believer to do in Christ's vineyard. There is work for children, there is work for young men, work for young women, and it is good to begin early. The Lord Jesus Christ, who was so pleased with the widow's mite (Luke 21:2–3), is very pleased with a child's love to him.

It is also good that when we begin to serve God, we should bear the yoke in another sense, namely, by finding difficulties. If it were in my power to make the way of serving Christ very easy to every young Christian here, I would not do it. If it were possible to make all Sunday-school work pleasant, I would not do it. If it were possible to make standing up in the open air to preach a very easy thing, I would not make it so. It is good for you that you bear the yoke. It is good that your service should involve self-denial and try your patience. It is good for you that the girls should not be very orderly, and that the boys should not be very teachable when you get them in the class. It is good for you that the crowd should not stand still and listen very meekly to you, and that infidels should put ugly questions to you when you are preaching in the street. It is good, I know, for the young minister to encounter curious church members, and even to meet with an adversary who means to overthrow him. It is a good thing for a true worker for the devil to labor to put him down, because if God has put him up, he cannot be put down, but the attempt to overthrow him will do him good, develop his spiritual muscle, and bring out the powers of his mind. A very easy path would not be profitable to us.

And it is good yet further. It is good to meet with persecution in your youth. If it were possible to take every young Christian and put him into a pious family and not let him go into the world at all, but always keep him in his mother's lap—if it were possible to take every working man and guarantee that he should only work in a shop where they sing psalms from morning to night, where nobody ever swears, where nobody ever utters a word of chaff against him—why, I say, if it were possible to do this, I do not know that it would be wise to do it. To keep people out of temptation is exceedingly proper, and none of us have any right to put a temptation in another's way; but it is good for us to be tempted sometimes, otherwise we should not know the real condition of our hearts and might be rotting with inward pride while blooming with outward morality. Temptation lets us know how weak we are and drives us to our knees. It tests our faith and tries our love and lets us see whether our graces are genuine or not.

Once more, I believe it is good for young Christians to experience much soul-trouble. My early days of thoughtfulness were days of bitterness. Before I found a Savior I was ploughed with the great subsoil plough of terrible convictions. Month after month, I sought but found no hope. I learned the plague of my heart, the desperate evil of my nature, and at this moment I have reason to thank God for that long wintry season. I am sure it was good to my soul. As a general rule, there is a period of darkness somewhere or other in the Christian life; if you do not have it at first it is probable you will not endure it again; but if you do not have it at first it is just as likely you will pass through the cloud at some other time. It is well to have it over. It is much better on the whole that a man should be timid and trembling than that he should early in life become very confident. "Blessed is the one that fears the LORD always" (Proverbs 28:14)—not the slavish fear, nor yet a fear that doubts God, but still a fear. There is a difference between doubting God and doubting yourself; you may have as much as you like of the last till you even get to self-despair, but there is no reason whatever why you should doubt the Lord.

These ordeals are of essential service to the newborn believer and prepare him alike for the joys and the sorrows of his spiritual career.

Day 22
Consolation for the Despairing

I had said in my alarm,
"I am cut off from your sight."
But you heard the voice of my pleas for mercy
when I cried to you for help.
Psalm 31:22

The man who wrote the verse before us was pained at his heart. There are many in like ease at this moment; their soul faints for heaviness, and their life is a burden. O you who are walking in the light deal gently with your brethren whose bones are broken, for you may also suffer from the like downcasting. Lay yourselves out to comfort the Lord's mourners. They are not good company, and they are very apt to make you unhappy as well as themselves, but for all that be very tender towards them, for the Lord Jesus would have you so. Remember what woes Ezekiel pronounces upon the strong who roughly push the weaker sort (Ezekiel 34:17–22). God is very jealous over his little children, and if the more vigorous members of the family are not kind to them, he may take away their strength, and make them even to envy the little ones whom once they despised. You can never err in being tender to the downcast. Lay yourself out as much as may be in you to bind up the broken-hearted and cheer the faint, and you will be blessed in the deed.

When the natural spirits sink in those men who have no God to go to, their depression takes its own particular shape. Any physician can tell you of instances of mental distress in which persons have surrounded themselves with imaginary ills and made themselves martyrs to fancied disorders. We have seen cases which might almost compel an observer to laugh if they had not been so terribly serious to the patients themselves. If a man be a Christian, it is very natural that his troubles should assume a spiritual form.

The only shades which can effectually darken his day are those which arise from sacred things; the fears which haunt him are not fears about his daily bread, but fears about the bread of life, fears as to his entrance into the eternal kingdom. The disease, from the physical side, is at bottom probably the same in the Christian as in the ungodly man, but, as his main thoughts are set upon divine things, he, in his depression, naturally dwells most upon his soul's affairs. At such times the spiritually afflicted are filled with horrible apprehensions.

What, let me ask you, is the most horrible apprehension that a Christian man can have? Is it not that of the text, "I am cut off from your sight"? Nothing distresses a Christian so much as the fear of being a castaway to God. You shall find no real Christian in despair because he is becoming poor, you shall not find him utterly cast down because worldly comforts are taken away; but let his Lord hide his face, and he is troubled; let him doubt his sonship, and he is overwhelmed; let him question his interest in Christ, and joy has fled; let him fear that the life of God never was in his soul, and you shall hear him mourn like a dove.

How can he live without his God? Yet this bitter sorrow has been endured by not a few of the best of men. If it could be said that only those Christians who walk at a distance from Christ, or those who are inconsistent in life, or those who are but little in prayer, have felt in this way, then, indeed, there would be cause for the gravest disquietude; but it is a matter of fact that some of the choicest spirits among the Lord's elect have passed through the Valley of Humiliation, and even sojourned there by the month together. Saints who are now among the brightest in heaven, have yet in their day sat weeping at the gates of despair, and asked for the crumbs which the dogs eat under the master's table (Matthew 15:27).

Read the life of Martin Luther. You would suppose, from what is commonly known of the brave reformer, that he was a man of iron, immovable and invulnerable; but on other occasions he sank to the very deeps, and was hard put to it to bear up at all, and that happened, too, even in his last moments, so that the worst battle of his life was fought upon that mysterious country which stretches towards the gates of the Celestial City. Do not condemn yourself, my dear sister, do not cast yourself away, my dear brother, because your faith endures many conflicts, and your spirits sink very low. David himself said in his haste, "I am cut off from before thine eyes," yet there sits David in the blessed choir in heaven, and even here on earth he was a man after God's own heart.

There are great benefits to come out of these severe trials and depressions.

There is a need for a season we should be in heaviness. You cannot make great soldiers without war, or train skillful seamen upon shore. It appears necessary that, if a man is to become a great believer, he must be greatly tried; if he is to be a great helper of others, he must pass through the temptations of others; if he is to be greatly instructed in the things of the kingdom, he must learn by experience; and if he is to be a loud singer to the tune of sovereign grace, he must hear deep calling unto deep at the noise of God's waterspouts. The uncut diamond has but little brilliance, the unthreshed corn feeds none, and so the untried professor is of small practical use or beauty. Many have a comparatively smooth pathway through life, but their position in the church is not that which the experienced believer occupies, neither could they do his work among the afflicted. The man who is much ploughed, and often harrowed, may thank God if the result of it is a larger harvest to the praise and glory of God by Jesus Christ. The time shall come with you whose faces are covered with sorrow, when you shall bless God for your sorrows; the day will come when you shall set much store by your losses and your crosses, your troubles and your afflictions, counting them happy which endure.

> From all your afflictions his glory shall spring,
> And the deeper your sorrows the louder you'll sing.

Day 23

The Thorn in the Flesh

So to keep me from becoming conceited because of
the surpassing greatness of the revelations,
a thorn was given me in the flesh, a messenger of Satan
to harass me, to keep me from becoming conceited.
2 Corinthians 12:7

We are plainly taught how mistaken we are when we set the eminent saints of the olden times upon a platform by themselves, as though they were a class of superhuman beings. Because we fall so far short of them, we excuse our indolence by conceiving them to be of a superior nature to ourselves, so that we cannot be expected to attain to their degree of grace. We elevate them upon a niche out of the way, so that they may not rebuke us, thus rendering them a homage which they never sought, and denying them a usefulness which they always coveted.

Indeed, this is a very injurious idea, and must not be tolerated. What the ancient saints were, we may be. They were men of like passions with ourselves, and therefore are most fit and practical examples for us. The Spirit of God which was in them is in all believers, and he is by no means straitened. Their Savior is our Savior; his fullness is the fullness out of which all of us have received. Let us put far away from us every notion of separating the holy men of former days from ourselves, as if they were a saintly caste to be admired at a distance, but not associated with as comrades. Paul, my brethren, doubtless enjoyed more revelations than we have done, but then he had a corresponding thorn in the flesh; he rises above us, but he sinks with us also, and so encourages us to emulate his rising.

The apostle says, "There was given to me a thorn." A thorn is but a little thing, and indicates a painful but not a killing trial—not a huge, crushing, overwhelming affliction, but a common matter; nonetheless painful, however, because common and insignificant. A thorn is a sharp thing, which pricks, pierces, irritates, lacerates, festers, and causes endless pain and inconvenience. Yet it is almost a secret thing, not very apparent to anyone but the sufferer. Paul had a secret grief somewhere, I know not where, but near his heart, continually wherever he might be, irritating him; perpetually vexing him and wounding him. A thorn, a commonplace thing, such as might grow in any field and fall to any man's lot. Thorns are plentiful enough, and have been since Father Adam scattered the first handful of the seed. A thorn—nothing to make a man remarkable, or give him the dignity of unusual sorrow. Some men boast about their great trials, and there is something in feeling that you are a man greatly afflicted; but a thorn could not drive even this wretched satisfaction. It was not a sword in the bones, or a galling arrow in the loins, but only a thorn, about which little could be said. Everyone knows, however, that a thorn is one of the most wretched intruders that can molest our foot or hand. Those pains which are despised because they are seldom fatal, are frequently the source of the most intense anguish—toothache, headache, earache, what greater miseries are known to mortals? And so with a thorn. It sounds like a nothing; "it can be easily removed with a needle," so those say who feel it not, and yet how it will fester; and if it remain in the flesh it will generate inconceivable torture. Such was Paul's trial;

a secret smarting, incessantly irritating, something—we do not know what.

It was a thorn "in the flesh." He was not tempted in the spirit; it was in the flesh. I suppose the evil had an intimate connection with his body. Many as the leaves of autumn have been the guesses of learned men, as to what Paul's thorn in the flesh was; almost every disease has had its advocates. I was particularly pleased to find that one scholar thought it to be the gout; but then other critics think it to be weak eyesight (Galatians 4:15, 6:11), stammering (1 Corinthians 1:17), or a hypochondriacal tendency. Richard Baxter, who suffered from a very painful disorder, which I need not mention, thought that the apostle was his fellow sufferer. One divine is of opinion that Paul endured the earache; and I generally find that each expositor has selected that particular thorn which had pierced his own bosom. Now, I believe that the apostle did not tell us what his peculiar affection was, that we may every one feel that he had sympathy with us—that we may every one believe that ours is no new grief. It was a trial mainly of the body, and from the use of the term "flesh," rather than "body," it would seem that it excited in the sufferer some fleshly temptation. It may not be so, but still, the writer is so accustomed to associate with "the flesh" the idea of sin, that I think it no idle conjecture that some temptation which the good man considered he had effectually overcome, fell upon him by reason of his bodily ailment; and it became, therefore, to him not merely a thorn in his flesh, but "a messenger of Satan," tempting him to an evil which he abhorred, and which for many a day had been so trampled down by his nobler nature, that he almost thought such a propensity extinct within him.

You see, brethren, that this thorn was well adapted to work out its design, for assuredly it would recall the apostle from ecstasies and excitements, and make him feel that he was in the body after all. He said once, "whether in the body or out of the body I do not know" (2 Corinthians 12:3), but when the thorn in the flesh was tearing him he soon settled that question. This made him feel he was a man, even as others. He had dreamed, perhaps, that he was growing very angelic, but now he feels intensely human. This made him feel only a man—that, though he was filled so full with God, still he was only a man, and could be filled as full with the devil, too, if deserted by grace. This made him know that he was a man in danger, and needed to fly to God for refuge; for here he was, ready to be exalted above measure even by divine blessings, and ready to be provoked into sin by the mere buffetings of an evil spirit.

Day 24

Sowing in the Wind, Reaping Under Clouds

He who observes the wind will not sow,
and he who regards the clouds will not reap.
Ecclesiastes 11:4

We are not to discard prudence in the choice of the time for our work. "For everything there is a season, and a time for every matter under heaven" (Ecclesiastes 3:1). It is well to sow when the weather is propitious. It is wise to "make hay while the sun shines." But Solomon here is pushing the other side of the matter. He had seen prudence turn to idleness; he had noticed some people wait for a more convenient season, which never came. He had observed sluggards making excuses, which did not hold water. So he, with a blunt word, generalizes, in order to make the truth more forcible. Not troubling about the exceptions to the rule, he states it broadly thus: "Take no notice of winds or clouds. Go on with your work whatever happens."

A man may observe the wind, and regard the clouds a great deal too much, and so neither sow nor reap. Note here, first, that in any work this would hinder a man. In any labor to which we set our hand, if we take too much notice of the difficulties, we shall be hindered in it. It is very wise to know the difficulty of your calling, the sorrow which comes with it, the trial which arises out of it, the temptation connected therewith; but if you think too much of these things, there is no calling that will be carried on with any success.

Poor farmers, they have a crop of hay and cannot get it in; they may fret themselves to death if they like, and never earn a penny for a seven years' fretting! We say of their calling that it is surrounded with constant trouble. They may lose everything just at the moment when they are about to gather it in. The seed may perish under the clods when it is first sown. It is subject to blight and mildew, and bird, and worm, and I know not what beside; and then, at the last, when the farmer is about to reap the harvest, it may disappear before the sickle can cut it.

Take the case of the sailor. If he regards winds and clouds, will he ever be put to sea? Can you give him a promise that the wind will be favorable in any of his voyages, or that he will reach his desired haven without a tempest? He that observes the winds and clouds, will not sail; and he that regards the clouds will never cross the mighty deep. If you turn from the farmer and the sailor, and come to the trader, what tradesman will do anything if he is always worrying about the competition, and about the difficulties of his trade, which is so cut up that there is no making a living by it? I have heard this, I think, about every trade, and yet our friends keep on living, and some of them get rich, when they are supposed to be losing money every year! He that regards the rise and fall of prices, and is timid, and will do no trading because of the changes on the market, will not reap. If you come to the workingman, it is the same as with those I have mentioned; for there is no calling or occupation that is not surrounded with difficulties.

In fact, I have formed this judgment from what friends have told me, that every trade is the worst trade out; for I have found somebody in that particular line who has proved this to a demonstration. I cannot say that I am an implicit believer in all I hear about this matter. Still, if I were, this would be the conclusion that I should come to, that he that observed the circumstances of any trade or calling, would never engage in it at all; he would never sow; and he would never reap.

Well now, dear friends, if there be these difficulties in connection with earthly callings and trades, do you expect there will be nothing of the kind with regard to heavenly things? Do you imagine that, in sowing the good seed of the kingdom, and gathering the sheaves into the garner, you will have no difficulties and disappointments? Do you dream that, when you are bound for heaven, you are to have smooth sailing and propitious winds all the voyage? Do you think that, in your heavenly trading, you will have less trials than the merchant who has only to do with earthly business? If you do, you make a great mistake. You will not be likely to enter upon the heavenly calling, if you do nothing else but unduly consider the difficulties surrounding it.

If we keep on observing circumstances, instead of trusting God, we shall be guilty of disobedience. God bids me sow; I do not sow, because the wind would blow some of my seed away. God bids me reap; I do not reap, because there is a black cloud there, and before I can house the harvest, some of it may be spoiled. I may say what I like; but I am guilty of disobedience. I have not done what I was bidden to do. I have made an excuse of the weather; but I have been disobedient. Dear friends, it is yours to do what God bids you do, whether the heavens fall down or not; and, if you knew they would fall, and you could prop them up by disobedience, you have no right to do it. What may happen from our doing right, we have nothing to do with; we are to do right, and take the consequences cheerfully. Do you want obedience to be always rewarded by a spoonful of sugar? Are you such a baby that you will do nothing unless there shall be some little toy for you directly after? A man in Christ Jesus will do right, though it shall involve him in losses and crosses, slanders and rebukes; yea, even martyrdom itself. May God help you so to do! He that observes the wind, and does not sow when he is bidden to cast his seed upon the waters, is guilty of disobedience.

Day 25

The True Christian's Blessedness

And we know that for those who love God all things work together for good, for those who are called according to his purpose.
Romans 8:28

Look around: above, beneath, and all things work. They work, in opposition to idleness. There is not a star though it seems to sleep in the deep blue firmament, which does not travel its myriads of miles and work; there is not an ocean, or a river, which is not ever working, either clapping its thousand hands with storms, or bearing on its bosom the freight of nations. There is not a silent nook within the deepest forest glade where work is not going on. Nothing is idle. The world is a great machine, but it is never standing still; silently all through the watches of the night, and through the hours of day, the earth revolves on its axis, and works out its predestinated course.

We are apt to think that the motion of the world and the different evolutions of the stars are but like the turning round of a child's windmill; they produce nothing. But things are not what they seem. Avalanche, hurricane, earthquake, are but order in an unusual form; destruction and death are but progress in veiled attire. Everything that is and is done, works out some great end and purpose. It is working out good for God's people.

I know, my brethren, it is very hard for you to believe this. "What!" say you? "I have been sick for many a day, and wife and children, dependent on my daily labor, are crying for food; will this work together for my good?" So says the Word, my brother, and so shall you find it ere long. "I have been in trade," says another, "and this commercial pressure has brought me exceedingly low, and distressed me: is it for my good?" My brother, you are a Christian. I know you do not seriously ask the question, for you know the answer of it. He who said, "all things work together," will soon prove to you that there is a harmony in the most discordant parts of your life. You shall find, when your biography is written, that the black page did but harmonize with the bright one—that the dark and cloudy day was but a glorious foil to set forth the brighter noontide of your joy. "All things work together."

Learn, then, that it is wrong to ask, concerning any particular act of providence, "is this for my good?" Remember, it is not the one thing alone that is for your good; it is the one thing put with another thing, and that with a third, and that with a fourth, and all these mixed together, that work for your good. Your being sick very probably might not be for your good; only God has something to follow your sickness, some blessed deliverance to follow your poverty, and he knows that when he has mixed the different experiences of your life together, they shall produce good for your soul and eternal good for your spirit. We know right well that there are many things that happen to us in our lives that would be the ruin of us if we were always to continue in the same condition. Too much joy would intoxicate us, too much misery would drive us to despair: but the joy and the misery, the battle and the victory, the storm and the calm, all these compounded make that sacred elixir whereby God makes all his people perfect through suffering, and leads them to ultimate happiness. "All things work together for good."

By "good," the Christian understands spiritual good. "Ah!" says he, "I do not call gold good, but I call faith good! I do not think it always for my good to increase in treasure, but I know it is good to grow in grace. I do not know that it is for my good that I should be respectable and walk in good society; but I know that it is for my good that I should walk humbly with my God (Micah 6:8). I do not know that it is for my good that my children should be about me, like olive branches round my table (Psalm 128:3), but I know that it is for my good that I should flourish in the courts of my God (Psalm 92:13), and that I should be the means of winning souls from going down into the pit. I am not certain that it is altogether for my good to have kind and generous friends, with whom I may hold fellowship; but I know that it is for my good that I should hold fellowship with Christ, that I should have communion with him, even though it should be in his sufferings (Philippians 3:10). I know it is good for me that my faith, my love, my every grace should grow and increase, and that I should be conformed to the image of Jesus Christ my blessed Lord and Master." Well, Christian, you have got upon the meaning of the text, then. "All things work together" for that kind of good to God's people.

And we may add, the text also means good eternal, lasting good. All things work together for a Christian's lasting good. They all work to bring him to paradise—all work to bring him to the Savior's feet. "And he brought them to their desired haven" (Psalm 107:30), said the psalmist—by storm and tempest, flood and hurricane. All the troubles of a Christian do but wash him nearer heaven; the rough winds do but hurry his passage across the straits of this life to the port of eternal peace. All things work together for the Christian's eternal and spiritual good.

And now I must return to the word "work"—to notice the tense of it. "All things work together for good." It does not say that they shall work, or that they have worked; both of these are implied, but it says that they do work now. All things at this present moment are working together for the believer's good. I can always believe the past, and always believe the future, but the present, the present, the present, that is what staggers faith. However troubled, downcast, depressed, and despairing, the Christian may be, all things are working now for his good.

Day 26

God Is with Us

What then shall we say to these things?
If God is for us, who can be against us?
Romans 8:31

There are four main enemies who conspire against the life of the children of God: there are man, the world, the flesh, and the devil. These always will be against us, but who are they?

First, there is man. How man has struggled against man! Man is the wolf of mankind. Not the elements in all their fury, nor the wild beasts of prey in all their cruelty, have ever been such terrible enemies to man as man has been to his own fellow. When you read the story of the Marian persecution in England, you are astounded that ever creatures wearing a human form could be so bloodthirsty. We do not in this age feel the cruelty of man to that extent, but this is only because the custom of the land will not allow it; for there are many who dare not smite with the hand, who are very busy in laying on their tongue, and this not by exposing our errors, which they have a perfect right to do, but in many cases the children of God are misrepresented, slandered, abused, persecuted, ridiculed for truth's sake; and we know many instances where other means are resorted to—anything to drive the servants of God away from their integrity and from their simple following of their Master.

The second adversary is the world. This world is like a great field covered with brambles, and thorns, and thistles, and as the Christian goes through it he is continually in danger of rending his garments or cutting his feet. Every child of God must march through the enemies' land, for Christ says, "I do not ask that you take them out of the world, but that you keep them from the evil one" (John 17:15). When is a Christian out of danger? Never. If he be prosperous, then he is apt to grow purse-proud or carnally secure; if adversities press upon him, then he is apt to murmur and to grow unbelieving. There are temptations in the high places of the earth, and the valleys are not without them.

There is a third enemy, and that is the flesh. It is the worst of the three. We should never need to fear man nor the world, if we had not this wicked flesh to carry about with us. Inbred corruption is the worst of corruption. "Lord," said Augustine, "deliver me from my worst enemy, that wicked man myself." If a Christian could lay himself down, and run away from himself, and never see himself again, he would be delighted beyond measure, for "I know that nothing good dwells in me, that is, in my flesh" (Romans 7:18), is the experience, not of the apostle only, but of every child of God.

The last enemy is the devil. I do not know whether he is worse than the flesh or not, but I think I may put him down as being about on a par with it; for when the devil meets our flesh, the two shake hands, and say, "How do you do, brother?" Truly the two are brethren—for our flesh was originally in the family of wrath. Ah! that arch-traitor Satan! little do we know what temptations he is plotting and planning for us even now. He is so crafty that he understands human nature better than human nature understands itself. He has been playing the trade of a tempter for six thousand years, he ought to be a thorough master of the business; and certainly he is.

But rejoice, Christian, whether it be man, or the whole world, or your flesh, or Satan, if God has predestinated you, called you, justified you, and in the person of Jesus Christ glorified you, you may put the whole together, and then say, "Who can be against us?"

God the Father cannot be against us. He is our Father; he cannot be against his own children; he has chosen us, he will not cast us away; he has adopted us into his family, he will never discard us; he has been pleased to ordain us unto eternal life, he will never reverse the decree. He was for us in the covenant of grace, when he planned the way to save rebellious man, he has been for us in the great ordering of providence—all things have worked together for good for us until now.

God the Son is not against us. O beloved, how sweetly he has been for us! I think I see him now, lifting up that face all covered with bloody sweat, and saying to every believer, "I am for you; these gouts of gore fall to the dust for you; I sweat great drops of blood that I might redeem you." I see him carrying the cross upon his bleeding shoulders, and every step he takes is to this tune, "I am for you." Today, as he pleads before the eternal throne, this is the tenor of his plea, "I am for you." When he shall come a second time without a sin-offering, unto salvation, the sound of the mighty trumpet which shall herald his advent, will ring out, "Christ is for you, O you blood-bought saints." When he shall sit upon the throne of his Father, and his kingdom shall come, whereof there shall be no end; this shall be the theme of that kingdom, "I am for my people; I will rule my people righteously, and bless the nations upon earth." Christ cannot be against you.

Then the Holy Spirit cannot be against us. He must always, as the Comforter, comfort his own people; as the Illuminator he must lead us into the truth; as the great Giver of Life he must always quicken us from our death of sin. Whatever power the Holy Spirit has, it is all engaged for us, "And behold, I am with you always, to the end of the age" (Matthew28:20).

So, Christian, whoever may be against you, here is a comfort: God the Father, God the Son, and God the Holy Ghost, never can be against you; and if it be so, who can be against you?

Day 27

The Lamb Is the Light

And the city has no need of sun or moon to shine on it,
for the glory of God gives it light, and its lamp is the Lamb.
Revelation 21:23

The inhabitants of the better world are independent of creature comforts. Let us think that over for a minute. We have no reason to believe that they daily pray, "give us this day our daily bread" (Matthew 6:11). Their bodies shall dwell in perpetual youth. They shall have no need of raiment; their white robes shall never wear out, neither shall they ever be defiled. They are satisfied by leaning upon God, needing not the creature for support. They need no medicine to heal their disease, "no inhabitant will say, 'I am sick'" (Isaiah 33:24). They need no sleep to recruit their fatigue, and although sleep is sweet and balmy—God's own medicine—yet they rest not day nor night, but unweariedly praise him in his temple.

They need no social ties in heaven. We need here the associations of friendship and of family love, but they are neither married nor are given in marriage there (Matthew 22:30). Whatever comfort they may derive from association with their fellows is something extra and beyond, they do not need any: their God is enough. They shall need no teachers there; they shall doubtless commune with one another concerning the things of God, and tell to one another the strange things which the Lord hath wrought for them, but they shall not need this by way of instruction; they shall all be taught of the Lord (Jeremiah 31:34), for in heaven "the glory of God gives it light, and its lamp is the Lamb." There is an utter independence in heaven, then, of all the creatures. No sun and no moon are wanted—nay, no creatures whatever.

Here we lean upon the friendly arm, but there they lean upon their beloved and upon him alone. Here we must have the help of our companions, but there they find all they want in Christ alone. Here we look to the meat which perishes, and to the raiment which decays before the moth (Matthew 6:19–20), but there they find everything in God. We have to use the bucket to get water from the well, but there they drink from the wellhead, and put their lips down to the living water.

Oh! what a blessed time shall that be, when we shall have mounted above every second cause and shall hang upon the bare arm of God! What a glorious hour when God, and not his creatures, God, and not his works, but God himself, Christ himself shall be our daily joy.

> Plunged in the Godhead's deepest sea,
> And lost in His immensity.

Our souls shall then have attained the perfection of bliss.

While in heaven, it is clear that the glorified are quite independent of creature aid, do not forget that they are entirely dependent for their joy upon Jesus Christ. He is their sole spiritual light. They have nothing else in heaven to give them perfect satisfaction but himself.

In heaven Jesus is the light in the sense of joy, for light is ever in Scripture the emblem of joy. Darkness betokens sorrow, but the rising of the sun indicates the return of holy joy. Christ is the joy of heaven. Do they rejoice in golden harps, in palm branches, and white robes? They may do so, but they only rejoice in these things as love-gifts from him. Their joy is compounded of this: "Jesus chose us, Jesus loved us, Jesus bought us, Jesus washed us, Jesus robed us, Jesus kept us, Jesus glorified us; here we are, entirely through the Lord Jesus—through him alone."

In glory they think of the character and person of Jesus, and these are wells of delight to them. Thus they muse—Jesus is eternal. God, his enemies reviled him, but still he is God. Jesus became the virgin's child; Jesus lived a life of holiness, and Jesus died; but see what triumph springs from his condescension and his shame: he rises, he ascends, and leads captivity captive; he scatters gifts amongst men; he reigns over earth, and hell, and heaven; King of kings, and Lord of lords.

They need no light of the sun and moon where Jesus is. However well the sun and moon may tell of God, we shall not want them from day to day to send forth their line throughout all the earth, and their word unto the end of the world, for the glory of Christ will teach us all we wish to learn; and beholding the unveiled glory of God will be better far than prying into the works of nature, even though we had an angel's power of discovery. We shall know more of Christ in five minutes, when we get to heaven, than we shall know in all our years on earth.

Christ in heaven is the great revealer of God's mind; and when he gets his people there, he will touch them with the wand of his own love, and change them into the image of his manifested glory. They were poor and wretched, but what a transformation! Their rags drop off and they are acknowledged as princes. They were stained with sin and infirmity, but one touch of his finger, and they are bright as the sun, and clear as crystal, transformed even as he was upon Mount Tabor, whiter than any fuller can make them. They were ignorant and weak on earth, but when he shall teach them, they shall know even as they are known. They were buried in dishonor, but they are raised in glory; they were sown in the grave in weakness, but they are raised in power; they were carried away by the hands of remorseless Death, but they arise to immortality and life.

In this sense Christ is the light of heaven, because it is through him that the true and real character of all the saints has been manifested.

Come, my soul, take wing a moment—it is not far for you to fly—mount up and walk the golden streets, and as you walk you shall see nothing but Jesus glorified. Come up to the throne, and you shall see Christ on it. Sit down and listen to the song, Christ is the theme; go to the banquet, Christ is the meat; mingle with the dancers, Christ is their joy; join in their great assemblies, Christ is the God they worship.

Day 28

The Departure

For I am already being poured out as a drink offering,
and the time of my departure has come.
2 Timothy 4:6

It is quite certain we shall not dwell here forever; we shall not live here below as long as the first man did, or as those fathers before the flood, who tarried some eight or nine hundred years. The length of human life then led to greatness of sin. Monstrosities of evil were ripened through the long continuance of physical strength, and the accumulating force of eager passions.

All things considered, it is a mercy that life is abridged and not prolonged to a thousand years. Amidst the sharp competition of man with man, and class with class, there is a bound to every scheme of personal aggrandizement, a limit to all the spoils of individual despotism, a restraint upon the hoardings of any one's avarice. It is well, I say, that it should be so. The narrow span of life clips the wings of ambition, and balks it of its prey. Death comes in to deprive the mighty of his power, to stay the rapacity of the invader, to scatter abroad the possessions of the rich. The most reprobate men must end their career after they have had their three score years and ten, or their four score years of wickedness.

And as for the good and godly, though we mourn their exit, especially when we think that they have been prematurely taken from us, we remember how the triumphs of genius have been for the most part achieved in youth, and how much the world has been enriched by the heads and hearts of those who have but sown the seeds of faith and left others to reap the fruits. If into less than the allotted term they have crowded the service of their generation, we may save our tears, for our regrets are needless. The summons will reach each one of us before long. We cannot stop here as long as the gray fathers of our race; we expect, and it is meet that we should prepare, to go.

The world itself is to be consumed one day. "The elements shall melt with fervent heat" (2 Peter 3:10 KJV). The land on which we stand we are wont to call "terra firma," but beneath it is probably an ocean of fire, and it shall itself feel the force of the ocean. We must not marvel, the house being so frail, that the tenants are unsettled and migratory. Certainly, whether we doubt it or not, we shall have to go. There will be a departure for us. Beloved believer in Christ Jesus, to you the soft term, "departure" is not softer than the truth it represents. To die is to depart out of this world unto the Father.

What say you about your departure? What say you of that from which you go, and what think you of that land to which you go? Well, of the land from which we go, my brethren, we might say many hard things if we would, but I think we had better not. We shall speak more correctly, if we say the hard things of ourselves. This land, my brethren, has been a land of mercy to us; there have been sorrows in it; but in bidding it farewell, we will do it justice and speak the truth concerning it. Our sorrows have usually sprung up in our own bosoms, and those that have come from the soil itself would have been very light if it had not been for the plague of our hearts, which made us vex, and fret over them. Oh, the mercy you and I have enjoyed even in this life! It has been worthwhile to live for us who are believers. Even had we to die like a dog dies, it has been worthwhile to live for the joy and blessedness which God has made to pass before us. I dare not call that an evil country in which I have met my Savior and received the pardon of my sin. I dare not call that an ill life in which I have seen my Savior, though it be through a glass darkly (1 Corinthians 13:12). How shall I speak ill of that land where Zion is built, beautiful for situation, the joy of the whole earth, the place of our solemn assemblies, where we have worshipped God? No; cursed of old as the earth was to bring forth the thorn and the thistle, the existence of the church of God in that land seems to a great degree to have made reparation for the blight to such as know and love the Savior.

Oh, have we not gone up to the house of God in company with songs of ecstatic joy, and have we not when we have gathered round the table of the Lord—though nothing was upon it but the type and emblem—have we not felt it a joyous thing to be found in the assembly of the saints, and in the courts of the Lord's house even here? When we bid farewell to earth, it shall not be with bitterness in the retrospect. There is sin in it, and we are called to leave it; there has been trial in it, and we are called to be delivered from it; there has been sorrow in it, and we are glad that we shall go where we shall sorrow no more. There have been weakness, and pain, and suffering in it, and we are glad that we shall be raised in power; there has been death in it, and we are glad to bid farewell to shrouds and to knells; but for all that there has been such mercy in it, such lovingkindness of God in it, that the wilderness and the solitary place have been made glad, and the desert has rejoiced and blossomed as a rose.

We will not bid farewell to the world, execrating it, or leaving behind us a cold shudder and a sad remembrance, but we will depart, bidding adieu to the scenes that remain, and to the people of God that tarry therein yet a little longer, blessing him whose goodness and mercy have followed us all the days of our life, and who is now bringing us to dwell in the house of the Lord forever.

Day 29
Our Light Affliction

For this light momentary affliction is preparing for us
an eternal weight of glory beyond all comparison.
2 Corinthians 4:17

Dear brethren and sisters in Christ, our affliction is light compared with the objects we have in view. Much of the affliction that the apostle had to endure came upon him because he was seeking the conversion of the heathen and the ingathering of the elect into the kingdom of Christ. If this is the object you also have in view, my dear friend, and you are made to suffer through your sedulous and faithful pursuit of it, I think you may truly call anything you have to endure a light affliction. If you have ever seen a mother sit up night after night with her sick child, you must have sometimes wondered that her eyes did not close in slumber. You were amazed that she did not permit someone else to share her task, but she seemed to think nothing of the cost to herself if she might only be the means of saving her little one's life. True love that made her labor light, and he who truly loves the souls of sinners will willingly bear any affliction for their sakes if he may but bring them to the Savior.

Yes, and he will also patiently endure affliction from them as he remembers how, in his own willfulness and waywardness, he caused his Savior to suffer on his behalf. If a man could know that, all through his life, he would have to wear a threadbare garment and exist upon very scanty fare; if he were sure that, throughout his life, he would meet with but little kindness from Christians, and with nothing but persecution from worldlings; and if, at the close of his career, he could only expect to be devoured by dogs or his body to be cast to the carrion crows, yet might he think all this to be but a light affliction if he might but win one soul from the unquenchable flame. Such trials as these are, happily, not necessary; but if they were, we might count them as nothing in comparison with the bliss of bringing up from the depths of sin the precious pearls that are forever to adorn the crown of the Redeemer.

Next, our affliction is light compared with our deserts. We can truly say, with the psalmist, "He does not deal with us according to our sins; nor repay us according to our iniquities" (Psalm 103:10). If the Lord had not dealt with us in mercy and in grace, we might have been at this moment beyond the reach of hope, like that rich man who in vain begged "Father Abraham" to send Lazarus to dip his finger in water to cool his parched tongue (Luke 16:24). Yes, ungodly one, you might have been in hell tonight, in that outer darkness where there is weeping and wailing and gnashing of teeth. Let the goodness of God in preserving you alive until now lead you to repent of your sin, and to trust in the Savior. Thank God, you are still out of the pit; the iron gate has not yet been opened to admit you, and then been closed upon you forever.

Then next, our affliction is very light compared with that of our Lord. Do you, dear friend, murmur at the bitterness of the draft in the cup which is put into your hand? But what heart can conceive of the bitterness of that cup of which Jesus drank? Yet he said, "shall I not drink the cup that the Father has given me?" (John 18:11). Is the disciple to be above his Master, and the servant above his

Lord? I think there is no consolation for an afflicted child of God so rich as that which arises from the contemplation of the sufferings of Jesus. The remembrance of the agony and bloody sweat of Gethsemane has often dried up the sweat of terror upon the anguished brow of the believer (Mark 14:32–36). The stripes of Jesus have often brought healing to his wounded followers. The thirst, the desertion, and the death on Golgotha—all the incidents of our Savior's suffering, and the terrible climax of it all (Mark 15:34)—have been most helpful in assuaging the sorrows of stricken saints. Brethren and sisters in Christ, your sufferings are not worth a moment's thought when compared with the immeasurable agonies of Jesus your Redeemer.

And further, beloved, our affliction is very light compared with the blessing which we enjoy. Many of us have had our sins forgiven, for Christ's sake, and the blessing of full and free forgiveness must far outweigh any affliction that we ever have to endure. When we were lying in the gloomy dungeon of conviction, and had not a single ray of hope to lighten the darkness, we thought that, even though we had to be kept in prison all our days, and to be fed only upon bread and water, we could be quite joyous if we could but be assured that God's righteous anger was turned away from us, and that our sins and iniquities he would remember against us no more forever. Well, that is just what many of us have experienced; our transgressions have been forgiven, and our sin has been covered by the great atoning sacrifice of Jesus Christ our Lord and Savior. Then let us rejoice and be glad all our days. But this is not all the blessing that we have received, for we have been clothed in the righteousness of Christ, and adopted into the family of God. Now we are heirs of God, and joint-heirs with Jesus Christ. We share even now in all the privileges of the children of God, and there are still greater favors and honors reserved for us in the future, as the apostle John said, “Beloved, we are God’s children now, and what we will be has not yet appeared; but we know that when he appears we shall be like him, because we shall see him as he is” (1 John 3:2). So it is quite true that, in comparison with our blessings and privileges, our affliction is indeed light.

Day 30

No Tears in Heaven

God will wipe away every tear from their eyes.
Revelation 7:17

It is an ill thing to be always mourning, sighing, and complaining concerning the present. However dark it may be, we may surely recall some fond remembrances of the past. There were days of brightness, there were seasons of refreshing from the presence of the Lord. Be not slow to confess, O believing soul, that the Lord has been your help! And though now your burden be very heavy, you will find an addition to your strength in the thought of seasons long since past, when the Lord lightened your load, and made your heart to leap for joy.

Yet more delightful will it be to expect the future. The night is dark, but the morning comes. Over the hills of darkness, the day breaks. It may be that the road is rough, but its end is almost in view. You have been clambering up the steep heights of Pisgah, and from the brow thereof you may view your glorious heritage (Deuteronomy 43:1). True the tomb is before you, but your Lord has snatched the sting from death, and the victory from the grave. Do not, O burdened spirit, confine yourself to the narrow miseries of the present hour, but let your eye gaze with fondness upon the enjoyment of the past, and view with equal ardor the infinite blessings of old eternity, when you were not, but when God set you apart for himself, and wrote your name in his book of life; and let your glance flash forward to the future eternity, the mercies which shall be yours even here on earth, and the glories which are stored up for you beyond the skies.

In heaven, Divine Love' removes all tears from the glorified. There are many reasons why glorified spirits cannot weep. These are well known to you, but let us just hint at them. All outward causes of grief are gone. They will never hear the toll of the knell in heaven. The coffin and the shroud are unknown things there. The horrid thought of death never flits across an immortal spirit. They are never parted; the great meeting has taken place to part no more. Up yonder they have no losses and crosses in business. "Therefore they are before the throne of God, and serve him day and night in his temple (Revelation 7:15)."

They know no broken friendships there. They have no ruined hearts, no blighted prospects. They know even as they are known, and they love even as they are loved. No pain can ever fall on them; as yet they have no bodies, but when their bodies shall be raised from the grave, they shall be glorified so that they shall not be capable of grief. The tear-gland shall be plucked away; although much may be there that is human, at least the tear-gland shall be gone, they shall have no need of that organ; their bodies shall be unsusceptible of grief; they shall rejoice forever. Poverty, famine, distress, nakedness, peril, persecution, slander, all these shall have ceased. "The sun shall not strike them, nor any scorching heat." "They shall hunger no more, neither thirst anymore" (Revelation 7:16), and therefore, well may their tears cease to flow.

Again, all inward evils will have been removed by the perfect sanctification wrought in them by the Holy Ghost. No evil of heart, of unbelief in departing from the living

God, shall vex them in paradise; no suggestions of the arch enemy shall be met and assisted by the uprisings of iniquity within. They shall never be led to think harshly of God, for their hearts shall he all love; sin shall have no sweetness to them, for they shall be perfectly purified from all depraved desires. There shall be no lusts of the eye, no lusts of the flesh, no pride of life to be snares to their feet. Sin is shut out, and they are shut in. They are forever blessed, because they are without fault before the throne of God. What a heaven must it be to be without spot, or wrinkle, or any such thing! Well may they cease to mourn who have ceased to sin.

All fear of change also has been forever shut out. They know that they are eternally secure. Saints on earth are fearful of falling, some believers even dream of falling away; they think God will forsake them, and that men will persecute and take them. No such fears can vex the blessed ones who view their Father's face. Countless cycles may revolve, but eternity shall not be exhausted, and while eternity endures, their immortality and blessedness shall coexist with it. They dwell within a city which shall never be stormed, they bask in a sun which shall never set, they swim in a flood tide which shall never ebb, they drink of a river which shall never dry, they pluck fruit from a tree which shall never be withered. Their blessedness knows not the thought, which would act like a canker at its heart, that it might, perhaps, pass away and cease to be. They cannot, therefore, weep, because they are infallibly secure, and certainly assured of their eternal blessedness.

Why should they weep, when every desire is gratified? They cannot wish for anything which they shall not have.

Eye and ear, heart and hand, judgment, imagination, hope, desire, will, every faculty shall be satisfied. All their capacious powers can wish they shall continually enjoy. Though "no eye has seen, nor ear heard, nor the heart of man imagined, what God has prepared for those who love him" (1 Corinthians 2:9), yet we know enough, by the revelation of the Spirit, to understand that they are supremely blessed. The joy of Christ, which is an infinite fullness of delight, is in them. They bathe themselves in the bottomless, shoreless sea of Infinite Beatitude.

Acknowledgments

This project would not have been possible without the involvement of many others. I'm grateful for the team at New Growth Press, including Brad Byrd and Ruth Castle, for their vision for creating devotional resources from church history. I'm also thankful for Jason Allen and the trustees at Midwestern Seminary for providing the time to work on resources to benefit the church. My assistants, David Aust, Isaac Pang, Olivia Hansen, and the other scholars who serve at the Spurgeon Library, helped with research, compiling, and editing. My church and my family have been a source of constant encouragement. Finally, I am grateful to God for his saving work in my life through his Son, Jesus Christ. May this volume give hope to his people amid suffering and glorify the Savior who will one day wipe away all our tears.